FROM ABSINTHE TO ABYSSINIA

FROM ABSINTHE

TO ABYSSINIA:

Selected Miscellaneous,
Obscure and Previously Untranslated
Works of Jean-Nicolas-Arthur Rimbaud

Translated by Mark Spitzer

CREATIVE ARTS BOOK COMPANY
Berkeley ⌐ California

Creative Arts Book Company
833 Bancroft Way
Berkeley, California 94710
800-848-7789
www.creativeartsbooks.com

Versions of these translations have appeared in *ACM, Exquisite Corpse, The Journal of African Travel-Writing, Mantis, The Adirondack Review, New Delta Review,* and *Lucid Moon.*

Library of Congress Cataloging-in-Publication Data

Rimbaud, Arthur, 1854-1891.
  [Selections. English. 2002]
  From Absinthe to Abyssinia: selected miscellaneous, obscure,
  and previously untranslated works of Jean-Nicolas-Arthur
  Rimbaud / translated by Mark Spitzer.
    p. cm.
  Includes bibliographical references.
  ISBN 0-88739-293-8 (alk. paper)
  I. Rimbaud, Arthur, 1854-1891—Translations into English. I.
Spitzer, Mark, 1965- II. Title.

PQ2387.R5 A2854 2002
841'.8--dc21

                            2002023344

Table of Contents

Acknowledgements

Knowingly or not
these people aided
in the mutation
of this book
I am glad:

Andrei Codrescu Rex Rose
Tom Maul Tina Vallery
Jack Peters Tami Carter
Jim Roderick Katherine McDonald
Mark Yakitch Ina Pfitzner
Emmanuelle Pourroy*
Anne Lhuillier*
Mark Jackson;
Dean Pyenson
ILL @ ULL
Skip Fox
George Whitman SARL
E.S. Rasmussen
Plamen Arnaudov
Don Ellis et al.
& Robin
Robin
Robin.

FROM ABSINTHE TO ABYSSINIA

Introduction

> **"I withheld the translation."**
> — Arthur Rimbaud,
> *Season in Hell*

When Rimbaud wrote "Oh gone life of mine, watch out!" (see "Scraps," p. 34), what he might have been referring to were the mistranslations of his works to come. Because that's what happened. Even the most accurate and faithful translators of Rimbaud (Louis Varèse, Wallace Fowlie and Oliver Bernard) have misunderstood the poetry, and consequently, have left less-than-accurate impressions of his work. For instance, Fowlie, in "O Seasons, O Castles," translates "chante le coq gaulois" (*crows the Gallic cock*) as "The Gallic cock grows."[1]

No doubt, this is a typographical error, but regardless of what kind of mistake it is, it has gone uncorrected for over thirty years. And there are plenty other such blunders in the translations of Rimbaud, thanks to the likes of Samuel Beckett, Ezra Pound, Charles Olson, Robert Lowell, Ben Belitt, Paul Schmidt, Delmore Schwartz, Mark Strand and more.

But it's not the obvious mistakes that matter; the ones that matter the most are those that go undetected. This is why no translation should ever be trusted, especially when the text is so complex that even the experts in the original language are stumped by multiple meanings, secret syntax and elusive argot. Such is the case with Rimbaud.

Hence, the surest way to approach a translation of Rimbaud is to know that we can only get as close as we can get. Meaning that for our clearest understanding of what Rimbaud meant in English, we must look to the translations with the least amount of dumb mistakes, which are the translations that hide these mistakes the best.

Misinterpretation, however, is the most important publicity a poet can hope for, especially when it leads to myth, thus attracting readers. In Rimbaud's case, his poems are read in English because his reputation is that of the adolescent rebel-genius who revolutionized poetry in France, then ran off to Abyssinia only to reappear twenty years later on his death-bed, a gun-running amputee rotting from a belt of gold he refused to take off. There's more to the story than this, of course, but I think it's fair to say that what interests readers of Rimbaud in languages other than French is not what he wrote, but what he didn't write, and what he did in the process of not writing what he didn't write.

My point is this: due to the distortion of myth, the English words *about* Rimbaud, up until the mid-1980s, have been just as unreliable as the English words *attributed to* Rimbaud, since they were woven with a tragic romanticism that made him out to be a fallen hero who flew too close to the sun. This image of the poet-martyr was mainly manifested by the pretentious biographer Enid Starkie, whose moralistic bias bent the facts, shaping our vision of Rimbaud. For example, Starkie insisted that Rimbaud traded in slaves because it was the colonial thing to do in Abyssinia at the time, an unsubstantiated view that was later modified due to the objections of other scholars.[2]

Then came decades of academics (spurred on by competition, argument for the sake of argument, and the fashion of refuting claims made by other critics), whose misinformation clashed with Starkie's. As a result, we now have a bunch of biographers who can't agree on what we don't know about Rimbaud; i.e., there's the argument that Madame Rimbaud encouraged her son's poetic practice and the argument that she didn't; there are those who contend that Rimbaud did drugs in Africa and those who claim the opposite; there's the debate over whether he was really gay; and there are numerous theories on what he died from (cancer, rheumatism, syphilis, dysentery, varicose veins, infection, etc.).

Hence, nobody knows Rimbaud. Not the experts, not his readers. Nobody.

⌇   ⌇   ⌇

What we do know about Rimbaud, though, and his statement about withholding the translation, is that it comes from his second "Delirium" section in *Season in Hell,* and was in reference to "a poetic language" he invented, "accessible, one day or another, to all the senses."[3] Meaning that the type of translation Rimbaud was referring to had nothing to do with going from French to any other language, but rather, had to do with translating the fabrications of his own delirium into a sublime new construct.

It was therefore left up to the translators to not only translate from the French, but from Rimbaud's deranged senses as well. This is something that nobody has done successfully yet, because all translations of Rimbaud are limited to literal interpretations. That's just the way it is when vowels have colors and alchemy is an allegory for the hallucination of words.

Nevertheless, the translators translated, often injecting guesswork that changed the tone of the original poems, leading readers in a false direction. Bertrand Mathieu, for instance, attempted to translate mood by substituting the hip lingo of the 60s for the eloquent vernacular of nineteenth-century France; in "Turned-On Morning" (his translation of "Matinée d'ivresse"), "mind-blowing jive" is substituted for "fanfare atroce," and the rest of the translation is just as much of a travesty.[4] Absurd translations like these, however, ultimately destroy their own credibility and cannot be taken seriously.

As Henry Miller noted in *The Time of the Assassins*, "In English we have yet to produce a poet who is able to do for Rimbaud what Baudelaire did for Poe's verse."[5] Half a century later, this still holds true: the pop translators of Rimbaud still have title-page disclaimers such as "plain translations in plain English" and "with plain prose translations of each poem," that attest to the failure commonly experienced when attempting a "poetic translation" of Rimbaud. Meanwhile, the minor translators have been more daring with their use of "poetic license," but haven't come up with much more than embarrassing renditions stylistically related to the school of Parnassian poetry mocked by Rimbaud for its flowery hypocrisy.

Hence, there are quite a few translations to choose from (including these), all of them suffering from the same problem as those that came before them: they were done out of interest, which is dangerous, because interest can lead to appropriation. And the moment that a translator starts to recreate a text in a way that he or she *believes* the author would approve of, that's the moment a work changes ownership. However, if a translation can retain the meaning of the original text as it innovates with form, then the translation remains faithful to the imagination of the poet.

from absinthe to abyssinia

Given this prerequisite, Postmodernism has recently provided a perspective on translation which regards the aesthetics of a secondary work in its own light. Modern translation theory holds that the original work must not be forgotten, overlooked or denied, and that a translation should be viewed as a companion to the original text.

This book is not bilingual, but the texts I selected are available, if anyone cares to go to the trouble of looking up my sources (listed in the back of the book). If people actually do this, however, they will no doubt wonder why I chose such obscure versions of the French to translate.

The reason for this has to do with personal taste. Since there are no reliable versions of the poems (editorial intrusion and mistranscription being well known in the works of Rimbaud), I decided to work on the works I liked best. Generally, these tended to be those with variations in vocabulary and oddities in punctuation that raised new questions about what Rimbaud really wrote. For example, the text I used in "Coppée Copy" (p. 47, line 9) employs the word "Filet," whereas other translators have chosen texts which use the word "Tibet" instead. Neither of these are known to be correct. Go figure.

꒯   ꒯   ꒯

After more than a century of affecting the landscape of poetry, it's amazing that a poet as vital as Rimbaud could have such an important body of work that has gone untranslated and unpublished in the English language up until now. I attribute this oversight to a general feeling of being content with what we think we know about Rimbaud. It's either this or ignorance (in the sense that we have been *ignoring* certain works, because they haven't yet been recognized for their literary merit).

This is not to say that this collection contains the entire remainder of the previously untranslated works of Rimbaud, because it doesn't. There are Latin compositions and other early works I chose not to translate, as well as some letters that I felt weren't worth the effort. I also left out some of the poems Rimbaud wrote during his underground Parisian days, which depend upon lists of names that wouldn't change in translation and would require extensive notation.

The previously untranslated works in this collection are as follows: "Dead Baby," "Jesus of Nazareth," "Invocation to Venus," "Three Kisses," some of the "Scraps," "Reconstructed Scraps," "Sketches of *Season in Hell*," the statements to the police, "Report on the Ogaden," "To the *Bosphore Égyptien*," and all the letters from Africa included in Part II.

Concerning the works from Africa, some briefly translated excerpts have appeared in secondary sources on Rimbaud and in dissertations and minor publications, but for the most part, these works are virtually unknown in the English language, since they never appeared in the three major translations of Rimbaud's alleged "collected" works (by Fowlie, Schmidt and Bernard).

Still, there are some works in this book that have been published in English before, like "Drunken Boat" and "Excerpts from *Season in Hell*." There is no logic as to why some poems were chosen and others were not. Some pieces, like "Bottom," were selected because of my affection for them. Others were chosen because I was curious and had always wanted to translate them. Beyond that, I looked for works that had never been seen in English before.

Concerning decisions made in the translating process (with the poetry in particular), I tried to avoid word choices

from absinthe to abyssinia

other translators had already used, unless the answer was so obvious that choosing an alternative (just for the sake of choosing an alternative) would have been transparent. In doing this, I often relied upon possibilities that had been overlooked by prior translators, but were no doubt intended by Rimbaud. Re-rendering Rimbaud's ideas by using words that came as close as possible to those originally used (in effect as well as definition, but not so much in sound) was always my main priority.

In all cases, translating style was a secondary concern. With form, however, I took some liberties. This is why some of the sonnets employ the nouveau experimental form uncommonly known as the *Spitzerian sonnet*. I will not explain my linebreaks or indentions, but will instead refer any interested parties to contemporary arguments on style in twentieth-century translation theory as posed by George Steiner in *After Babel* and demonstrated by Ted Berrigan in his innovative translation "The Drunken Boat" (in which the text was lifted from Varèse, but presented with stylistic difference).

In the poems, I chose to mainly go the route of free-verse. As American poetry has recently discovered, alliteration and assonance can substitute their movement for the passé momentum of rhyming — a conventional technique Rimbaud applied, even though he taught the French that they didn't need to practice such linguistic trickery anymore.

As for punctuation, I did not withhold the translation. Rimbaud, especially in his letters, tends to use dashes and commas (sometimes together) to create run-on sentences that don't always work as well in English as they do in French. For the sake of consistency, I shortened some sentences by breaking them up, but others I let ramble. Also, there are quite a few unnecessary commas, colons and semi-colons (especially at the end of line-breaks in the poems), which I deleted because I felt they added an extraneous and controlling tone to the American English used in these translations. In the same vein, I cut down on the amount of exclamation marks (particularly in "Drunken Boat"), while retaining many of the capitalizations sometimes added for emphasis.

In Rimbaud's more formal prose, used in his reports and letters from Africa, I employed less liberties than I did with the poems. Since Rimbaud, at this point, was no longer writing poetic manifestos, there didn't seem to be any reason to reflect a lyrical tone.

These translations are meant to be as accurate as possible in imagery and idea, as opposed to being exact with every single article, conjunction, pronoun, etc. One of the foremost things a translation should do is flow smoothly, meaning that sometimes a translator needs to do some tweaking to keep the reader from stumbling. Without changing anything integral, this was my goal. I believe that I have been faithful to the intention of these works, except for some occasional and additional acrobatics in the verse to make up for the unavoidable loss in music that occurs when going from French to English.

$$\mathit{\smallsmile} \qquad \mathit{\smallsmile} \qquad \mathit{\smallsmile}$$

Part II of this book is made up of works Rimbaud wrote during a time when he was concerned with information. Many of these works are letters that other translators, for whatever reasons, neglected to put into English. Some business letters, however, were left out of this collection due to tedious details regarding merchandise and records of payment, whereas other letters

from absinthe to abyssinia

were edited into excerpts, to exclude extraneous lists of items and prices. For the most part, though, this selection completes the English corpus of Rimbaud's known epistolary history.

Without doubt, "Report on the Ogaden" and "To the *Bosphore Égyptien*" are the most crucial pieces in this book. How they escaped translation for over a century is baffling, since they are the main works of one of France's greatest writers during the second half of his life. Also, these reports are historically significant, not only because they show who Rimbaud created himself into, but because they are some of the first reports by a European explorer from the African interior.

But what these works of prose do best is give us a clearer idea of what Rimbaud was doing in Abyssinia when he wasn't conducting business or exploring uncharted regions. Contrary to popular belief, he did not give up writing; but he did give up poetry in favor of a less-idealistic approach to his passion — which he reportedly threw himself into, shutting himself up for days in his hut, writing as if possessed. He may not have written as frantically as when he was young, ranting and raving in the family barn, but he was prolific as an adult, amassing more pages of prose in Africa than poetry ever written in France.

Still, the question remains: *Did Rimbaud give up writing?* This is because most readers of Rimbaud prefer a genius driven to the abyss by madness, rather than a capitalist who switched to journalism. Or a hermit who studied languages, but hardly used them. Or an amateur scientist who discovered nothing.

Science: it's a subject he mocked in *Season in Hell*, but aspired to in Africa. Rimbaud was obsessed with the study of mechanics. He was constantly requesting geological equipment, and ordering books on architecture and construction through his mother. He fiddled with photography, metals, chemicals, etc., and noted that if he ever had a son he would raise him to be an engineer.[6]

Whether this fascination with the facts arose through his disillusionment with poetry, or whether he actually had an aptitude for working with numbers and figures, is not certain. What we do know is that this desire to work with the physical world became apparent in his writing, as his work became more clinical and detached from the realm of emotion. In place of bashing religion, questioning his sexuality and embracing ennui, he wrote about history, economics, geography and commerce.

This is information, of course, that scholars of Rimbaud have always known. In the last couple decades, though, our understanding of Rimbaud has changed considerably. With the publication of several studies that focus on the post-poet Rimbaud (i.e., *Rimbaud in Abyssinia* by Alain Borer, and *Somebody Else: Arthur Rimbaud in Africa* by Charles Nicholl), the earlier, more romantically-inclined biographies, depicting him as a visionary mystic, have been replaced by books that take a more objective look at a man who would no doubt prefer a more objective approach to the history of literature.

Hence, more than ever before, the evidence exists that Rimbaud was not a poet, but ultimately, a businessman who wrote travel literature. Moreover, we are deceiving ourselves if we continue to perpetrate the falsehood that Rimbaud was a slave-trader, for as recent literature on Rimbaud has made clear, slavery was illegal in Abyssinia at the time, even though slaves from other places were brought into the region or employed as domestics. As Rimbaud's own letters indicate, despite his non-committal inquiries into the trafficking of slaves, Rimbaud, even in his most elitist and condescending moments, was known for his fair treatment of workers. Furthermore, people who knew him at the time described him as compassionate to the indigenous, especially in his intimate relations with native women whom he apparently treated with respect. And then there's Djami, his native servant-boy and suspected lover, whom he left an inheritance to. But definitely, if Rimbaud ever traded in slaves, there would have been records, of which he left plenty.

What Rimbaud did trade in were guns, coffee, fabric, pots and pans, etc. But he wasn't a very good wholesaler, since the place he chose to conduct his business presented so many obstacles that he wasn't left with much to show for his efforts except a long list of misadventures leading to his death, and an incredible story.

Therefore, if these new translations can give us anything, what they offer most is some balance in what we know about Rimbaud, in relationship to what we pretend to know and what we have misunderstood. Nevertheless, misunderstandings are important because they play a key role in maintaining myth, thus providing future poets (who have the potential to explode old ways) with a model they can relate to and apply to their own work. Not that it's likely that we shall ever see another poet like Rimbaud, who changed the face of poetry 130 years ago, but at least such aspirations feed the revolutionary, evolutionary machinery of verse — which can fool us if we want it to, bring a nation to its knees, inspire a generation, or perhaps, do nothing at all.

— Mark Spitzer
Baton Rouge
2001.

End Notes

1. See Rimbaud, Arthur. *Rimbaud: Complete Works, Selected Letters*. Trans. Wallace Fowlie. Chicago: University of Chicago Press, 1966, pp. 150–151.

2. For more information on Starkie's intentional misinformation regarding Rimbaud and slavery, see Nicholl, Charles. *Somebody Else: Arthur Rimbaud in Africa, 1890–91*. London: Jonathan Cape, 1997, pp. 281–282.

3. Rimbaud, Arthur. "Deliriums II, Alchemy of the Word." *A Season in Hell/The Illuminations*. Trans. Enid Rhodes Peschel. New York: Oxford University Press, 1973, p. 77.

4. See Rimbaud, Arthur. "Turned-On Morning." *A Season in Hell & Illuminations*. Trans. Bertrand Mathieu. Rochester, NY: BOA Editions, 1991, p. 107.

5. Miller, Henry. *The Time of the Assassins: A Study of Rimbaud*. New York: New Directions, 1956, p. vi.

6. For example, see Rimbaud's letter of May 5, 1884, in Fowlie's *Rimbaud: Complete Works, Selected Letters*, pp. 342–343.

from absinthe to abyssinia

PART I

POETRY

JUVENILIA

1865–1870

Zounds[1]

I

The sun was still warm, though it hardly lit the earth anymore. Like a torch placed before a gigantic vault, it lit it with a faint glow. Thus, the sun, terrestrial torch, allowed one last faint glimmer to escape its flaming body as it began to extinguish, allowing green leaves to be seen again, along with tiny fading flowers, the incredible summit of the pines, the poplars and the ancient oaks. The refreshing wind, or rather, the breeze, shook the leaves with a rustling like a silvery stream flowing at my feet. The ferns were bowing their green heads in the wind. And I fell asleep, but not before drinking from the stream.

II

I dreamed... I was born in Reims in 1503.

Reims was a small town then, or rather, a trading center famous for its beautiful cathedral that witnessed the Coronation of King Clovis.

My parents were not very rich, but they were honest. They didn't have more than a small house which they owned for twenty years before I was born, plus a few thousand francs and some change put away by my mother.

My father was an officer in the Royal Guard. He was a tall, thin, dark-haired man with the same colored eyes and beard and skin. Although he wasn't even 48 or 50 when I was born, he could have easily been mistaken for 58 or 60. He had a quick, explosive temper and was frequently enraged. He refused to put up with anything that did not please him.

My mother was quite different: a sweet, peaceful woman, not upset by much, who kept the house in perfect order. She was so serene that my father used to treat her like a young lady. But I was loved the most. My brothers were less brave than me, even though they were bigger. I didn't like studying; that is, reading, writing and arithmetic — but when it came to picking up the house, gardening and running errands.... No problem! I liked that.

I remember one day when my father promised me twenty sous if I would do a division problem for him. I began, but could not finish. Oh, he often promised me centimes, toys, candy, and once he even promised me five francs if I would read something to him. Nevertheless, he sent me to school as soon as I was ten. Why, I would ask myself, learn Latin and Greek? I don't know. Nobody really needs it! So what if I pass my exams? What's the use in passing exams? Nothing, that's what! But there is a use: You can't find a job unless you pass your exams, so they say. But I don't want a job. I will be a rich man. But even if you wanted a job, why learn Latin? Nobody speaks that language anymore. Sometimes I see Latin in the newspapers. Thank God I will never be a journalist!

And why learn geography and history? It's true we need to know that Paris is in France, but no one ever asks what latitude it's on. And history: to learn about the lives of Chinaldon, Nabopolasser, Darius, Cyrus and Alexander, and to learn the diabolical names of all their remarkable compatriots — it's torture.

from absinthe to abyssinia

So what if Alexander was famous?... So what if we know the Latins existed? Their language is probably some language they copied. And even if they did exist, they should just let me be rich, and they should keep their language to themselves! What have I done to them that they should put me to such torture? Let's move on to Greek. No one speaks that filthy language, no one in the world!...

Zounds! I will be rich instead. Sitting around on your rear isn't good for anything! Zounds!

To be a shoeshine boy — to attain the position of a shoeshine boy — you have to pass an exam, because the only job you're going to get is that of shoeshine boy. Or a herder of cows and pigs. Zounds again! I don't want any of that! The only compensation you'll ever get for that is a smack in the ears. They'll call you an animal, which isn't true. They'll say you're only half a man, etcetera.

Oh! Zounds, Zounds, Zounds!...

(To be continued)

Arthur

Dead Baby[2]

The first day of the new year was already over
        (a nice day for children, so longly awaited
        so quickly forgotten).
Deep in smiling slumber... the sleeping child is silent
lying in his downy cradle, his noisy rattle on the floor.
He remembers it and happily sleeps.
After receiving presents from his mother, he gets some from
        the dwellers of Heaven.
His smiling mouth begins to open; his half-open lips
        look as if they're calling to God.
Near his head an Angel leans over him
spying on the delicate murmurs of an innocent heart
staring at his celestial face, admiring the pleasure
in his peaceful brow, and his soul, that flower
which has never felt the southern wind:

        "Child who looks like me
Come, rise into the sky with me!
Enter into the celestial kingdom
live in the palace you've seen in your dreams
you are worthy of it! May the earth never keep
a child from heaven! No one can trust
anyone on earth — mortals never find
true happiness there.
From the scent of flowers
something bitter rises
restless hearts only know sad joy
pleasure can't be felt without any clouds
a tear glimmers in ambiguous laughter.
A bitter life would make the pureness fade from you
worries would confuse the tears in your blue eyes
dark shadows would chase the pinkness from your face.

        from absinthe to abyssinia

No! You will enter holy realms with me
and your voice will join in the choir of Heaven.
You will watch over men and their troubles here.
Come! Something divine is breaking the chains
binding you to life.
May your mother never wear a veil of mourning!
May she never see your coffin, only your cradle!
May she banish sad smiles
and may your funeral never
darken her face, but rather
may she bring handfuls of lilies to your wake
for the last day of an innocent being
is always his most beautiful!"

Swiftly and delicately, the angel puts his wing
to the rosy mouth of the child, to reap him unaware
and receives the soul of the harvested child
which he takes to higher places
gently flapping his azure wings.

Now the cradle holds only pale limbs
that still retain their beauty
even though the vital breath
doesn't nourish nor provide
life anymore. He is dead...
And from his lips still scented with kisses
the name of his mother
lingers as laughter
expires and he dies
recalling his gifts this first day of the year.
His heavy eyes seem to be shut in peaceful sleep
haloing his head with mysterious celestial light
which is more than just a mortal honor;
it attests that he is no longer an earthly child
      but a heavenly one.

Oh! The tears she cries for the loss of her child!
She bathes his precious grave in tears!
But each time she shuts her eyes to sleep
a little Angel appears to her in the rosy sky
where he calls to her, cheerfully.
They smile at each other as he glides through the air.
On snowy wings he circles his astounded mother
then divinely kisses
her lips
      with his.

Rimbaud Arthur
Born October 20, 1854
in Charleville.

from absinthe to abyssinia

Jesus of Nazareth[3]

Jesus once lived in Nazareth.
He grew in virtue as he grew in age.
One morning when the village roofs were glowing red
he got out of bed when everything was deep in sleep
so that when Joseph arose he'd find his work done.
Pushing and pulling a giant saw
his youthful arms cut planks
as he bent above his work
with a tranquil expression
while faraway, the shining sun
appeared above the lofty mountains
its flaming silver entering
the humble windows...
Then came the cattlemen leading their herds to pasture
and as they passed the young worker and the sounds
of morning work
they asked:

> "Who is this child? His face is gravely beautiful
> strength is bursting from his arms.
> Like a highly skilled worker
> he cuts the cedar artfully.
> Even in the days of yore
> Hiram never worked so passionately
> when he cut with huge toiling hands
> the great cedars and beams of the temple
> before Solomon, yet
> the bending body of this child
> swinging his axe straight from the shoulder
> is more supple than a reed."

His mother, hearing the grating of the blade
gets out of bed
and softly, in silence, goes to him.
She nervously glimpses him working hard
maneuvering enormous planks.
Lips shut tight
she watches him serenely
indistinct words quiver on her lips
laughter sparkles in her tears...
but then the saw breaks, injuring his fingers
staining the white robe
of the unsuspecting child
with purple blood...
a slight cry escapes his mouth.
Then suddenly he sees his mother
so hides his reddened fingers
underneath his clothes
pretending to smile as he greets her.

. . . .

She throws herself at his feet — Alas! —
She holds his fingers in hers
kissing his tender hands and moaning
her face bathed in tears.
But the child is unmoved:

> "Why are you crying, unknowing mother?
> Because the saw grazed my finger?
> The time has not yet come
> for you to cry!"

Resuming his work
his completely pale mother
quietly turns her face toward the ground
then looking sadly
up at her son
   says: "God Almighty,
     may Thy will
     be done!"

    1870

            A. Rimbaud

Mother of the sons of Aeneas, oh delights of the Gods
delights of mortals, beneath the stars of heavens
Venus, you populate everything: the waves of floating boats
and the fertile soil. Through you every breathing being
sprouts, stands and sees the shining sun!
You appear... Dark clouds and wind disappear
at the sight of your radiant face...
the Ocean smiles at you: abundant with beautiful work.
The Earth spreads flowers beneath your feet
and daylight shines even purer beneath the azure!
As soon as April returns full of youth
ready to bring tenderness to everything
the zephyr's breath escapes its prison
and the ethereal people announce your season:
The charmed bird bows before your power, oh Goddess
wild animals leap through lush grass
cleaving the sea as they swim
as all living creatures shackled to your grace
burn as they pursue you!
Through the seas, torrents, mountains and fields
through forests thick with nests
you pour your powerful precious love
into the heart of everything
to propagate their blood
through the ages!
Venus, the world knows nothing but your empire!
Without you nothing could rise to see the day
Without you there is no inspiration or experience of love!
I aspire to your divine presence in my work!...

Three Kisses[5]

She was barely dressed
as huge trees indiscreetly
reached their leaves maliciously
very very close to the window.

Sitting half-naked in my chair
she was clasping her hands
while her little feet shuddered
with joy on the floor.

Pale as wax
I watched a tiny renegade ray
flutter in her smile
and then on her breasts
like a fly upon a rose.

I kissed her ankles
as her laughter assailed me
in clear soft
crystalline
trills.

Her delicate feet fled beneath her gown:
    "Will you stop it!"
My act of brashness having been permitted
she was pretending to punish me.

With pathetic quiverings in my lips
I softly kissed her eyes.
Daintily she threw back her head:
    "Sir, you're going too far!
    I must inform you..."

I gave her the rest
in the breasts
as she laughed
at my kisses
willingly...

She was barely dressed
as huge trees indiscreetly
reached their leaves maliciously
very very close to the window.

from absinthe to abyssinia

POETRY AFTER 1870

I

Beneath dark walls, beating skinny dogs...

II[7]

Oh! Just as bells are made of bronze
our hearts are full of despair!
In June 1871
slaughtered by a dark creature
we, Jean Balouche and Jean Baudry
having achieved our desires
died in that ambiguous belfry
detesting Desdouets!

III

Jerking with gruesome hiccups from behind
a swallowed rose in the doorman's belly.

IV

A brunette was sixteen when they married her off
. . . .
so she fell in love with her son of seventeen.

V

[Complaint of the Old Monarchist
To Monsieur Henri Perrin, Republican Reporter]

. . . .
. . . . You have lied
upon my thighs, you have lied! You stinking apostle!
Do you want to turn us into bums?
Do you want to skin us alive?
I have two twisted deformed thighs!

Every day at the college
you sweat enough to fry a fritter
on your collar!

And you lie through your teeth
like a worn-out horse
slobbering at the mouth!
You'd like to wipe away my forty years of office!

But I've got my thighs! I've got my thighs! I've got my
thighs!
For forty years I've been twisting
on the hard edge of my beloved walnut chair
the impression of the wood is always there
and when I see your filthy organ
and all your subscribers
gripping it
. . . .
I'll just keep working forever on these thighs
that I've been forming for the last forty years
you clown!

VI

[The Grocer's Lament]

If only he'd come into the store when the blue glass moon
    is shimmering
If only he'd swipe a can of chicory
    in front of me.

VII

. . . . Is it
. . . . (some barrels?) . . . . . getting busted?
. . . . No!
It's a head chef snoring like a bassoon.

VIII

. . . . Among the gold and quartz and porcelain
. . . . a vulgar chamberpot
the indecent reliquary of noble old ladies
squatting shamefully above the royal mahogany.

IX

Oh! Perennial vignettes!

X^8

And the drunken poet was raving at the Universe.

XI

Softly on the plains it rains.

XII

Oh gone life of mine, watch out!

XIII

Moonlight, when the bell struck twelve...

Iranian Caravan Scrap

When the Iranian caravan stopped at the fountain of Ctési-phon, it was with the despair of finding it drained. Some accused the Magis, others the Muslim priests. The camel drivers cursed together . . . They had been traveling for several moons . . . with cargos of incense, gold and myrrh. Their leader cried out . . . decided to eliminate . . . Some accepted.

All the cloaky overcoats
protect a musky butt
as vulcanized leggings
truss up a fat knee.

To the apoplectic grocers
I'll give a carnivorous taste.
So much acrobatic practice
has endowed me with an iron member.

My hard leg painted with bile
will make the wooden bowl resound
with a calculated kick in the ass.

Ah! I prefer an Asian fruit
the apple that Adam grabbed
soaked in a vat of brass.

*Reconstructed Scraps I*⁹

from absinthe to abyssinia

But finally, understand, tonight
having given up all hope
I have the option to stop
and retire from the world;
to dream serenely; to see
the picture of Christ surrounded
by sweet untroubled animals;
And far from your atrocities —
the vapid elaboration
of a damning
Cholera.

Damninetics[10]

YOUNG GLUTTON[11]

Silk cap
ivory prick
dark attire

Paul eyes
the cupboard
sticks his

tiny tongue
to pear
prepares

his baguette
and shits
himself.

Wretch
drinking:
Vision
pearling:

Stupid
law!
Carriage
tipping!

Woman
falling:
Loins

bleeding:
Bitching
bleating!

In Rome, at the Sistine Chapel
covered with Christian emblems
there's a scarlet casket where
some ancient noses wither:

Ascetic noses of ancient Egypt
priestly noses of the Holy Grail
where the livid night hardens
along with an ancient
sepulchral plainsong.

And every morning
into this mystic dryness
schismatic filth goes in
reduced to fine dust.

[Parody of Léon Dierx]

As on Sunday evenings
there are bluish roofs
and white doors:

At the end of the soundless city
the Street is white
it is night.

There are strange houses
on the Street
with angels on their blinds.

But suddenly
a little black Cherub
comes running

rigidly
and wickedly
toward a stone post

staggering
having eaten too many
jelly beans.

He takes a poop then disappears
but beneath the holy
empty moon

his damned poop appears
in a little cesspool
filthy with blood!

[Parody of Louis Ratisbonne]

Oh enema! Oh lily! Oh silver douche!
Spiteful of work, spiteful of famine!
The dawn fills you with a cleansing love!
A heavenly sweetness butters your stamen!

[Parody of Armand Silvestre]

Parody of Louis-Xavier de Ricard[12]

Humanity buggered the immense child Progress.

Scapin
escaping
scratches
a rabbit
underneath
his overcoat.

Colombina
— *Do, re, mi, fa* —
got screwed!

patting the eye
of the rabbit slut
getting drunk...

[Parody of Paul Verlaine]

MEMORIES OF A STUPID OLD MAN

Forgive me, Father!
For I was young, at the fair, and searching
not for that stupid shooting gallery where every shot's a winner
but for that place of shouting where donkeys
with tired flanks display that long cruel tube
which I still don't understand!...
                                        And then my mother
whose nightgown had a bitter odor
and was frayed at the bottom and yellow as fruit
climbed into bed with a grunt
But I was a hardworking son — and my mother
with her ripe thighs and fat butt
where the linen scrunches up
got me unspeakably hot!...

But a cruder calmer shame was when
my little sister after school
having worn out her clogs on the ice long ago
was pissing and watching
a delicate thread of pee beneath her
escape her tight pink lips!...

Oh forgive me!
                    I have even imagined my father:
At night, during card games, the filthiest words...
the neighbor kid and I kept getting shoved away
        due to things seen...
For a father is disturbing!...
        due to things conceived!...
Sometimes I fondled his knee... my fingers wanted
to open his fly — oh! no! —
to have that fat hard dark dick
of my dad, whose hairy hand cradled me!...
                        I can't talk
About that chamberpot I saw in the attic
the forbidden books, the basket of lint
the Bible, the toilets, the maid
the Holy Virgin and the crucifix...
                    Oh! Nobody
was really bothered as much as they were shocked!
And now, may forgiveness be granted to me:
Since the sickening senses have made me their victim
I confess to the crimes of youth!...

. . . .

Next! — If I may be allowed to speak to the Lord! —
Why belated puberty and the problem of the stubborn
domineering dick? Why slow shadows
at the bottom of the belly? And those countless terrors
which always bury my joy in black gravel?
Always I've been stupefied! What's there to know?

. . . .

Am I forgiven?...
        O Father, give me back the blue booties of my youth! . . . .
. . . .
. . . . — and let's jerk off together!

[Parody of François Coppée]

from absinthe to abyssinia

COPPÉE COPY[14]

On summer nights beneath the blazing storefront eye
when sap shudders in blackened gutters
radiating under the slender chestnut trees
I watch dark groups of domestic men
suck on pipes and pucker cigs
in the urinals where I wander
as chocolate ads glow redly above
and I imagine how the winter will freeze
my babbling Channel
which soothes the human sea
while the harsh north wind
spares no vein.

[Parody of François Coppée]

The poor messenger beneath the canopy of tin
warming an enormous chilblain in his glove
shoves a money-sack away from his swollen groin
as he follows a fat whore along the left-bank Seine.
Meanwhile there are gendarmes lurking in soft shadows
while honesty inside watches the moon
in the deep of the sky, cradled in green fleeciness
despite the curfew and the dangerous hour
as the whore returns to Odeon, defiled
and a wretch barks out
in the darkened square!

[Parody of François Coppée]

MELANCHOLY HYPERIMAGISM, AFTER BELMONTET

What then is this mystery, impenetrable and dark?
Why, without displaying its dark white sail
is any royal young skiff rigged?

Let's reverse the grief of our tears —
. . . .
       Love wants to live at the expense of its sister
       Friendship lives at the expense of its brother
. . . .
The scepter which is hardly revered
is only the cross of a great shrine
atop the volcano of nations!
. . . .
Oh! Honor was dripping upon your manly mustache.

> [Parody of an archetypal poem
> of the Parnassian school of poetry]

To the peasants of the emperor!
To the emperor of the peasants!
To the son of Mars!
To MARCH 18th the glorious!
When Heaven blessed Eugénie's womb!

from absinthe to abyssinia

Because this seat was built so badly
that it makes our entrails roil
this hole was no doubt masoned
by real scoundrels.

When the notorious murderer Troppmann destroyed Henri Kink
he must've sat upon this throne
since those idiots, Henry V and Napoleon III
truly deserve this seat
in this state
of siege.

Drunken Boat

Descending Rivers of indifference
the tug of towmen
to stakes painted
using men

        I no longer felt
caught and nailed naked
       by raving Redskins
         as targets.

I didn't care
bearing Belgian wheat
when the haulers finished
the Rivers sent me

about any crew
or English cotton
screaming away
on my way.

Last winter in the furious
I fled more oblivious
drifting Peninsulas
more victorious

       slap of the tide
than in a child's mind
    never knew chaos
       than mine.

The storm blessed
lighter than a cork
known as the eternal
for ten nights, longing not

my awakenings at sea
I danced upon the waves
rollers of the dead
for the light of men.

Sweeter than sour
green water broke through
washing off stains
sweeping my anchor

     apple flesh to a child
       my pinewood hull
of vomit and blue wine
    and rudder away.

And ever since then
has been bathing me
devouring the green azure
sometimes sink

the Poem of the Sea
infused with milky stars
where sulking victims
in pale enraptured fathoms.

from absinthe to abyssinia

Where sudden in
delirium and rhythms slow
superior to lyres)
fermenting the bitter

the glow of day
(more powerful than alcohol
taint the blues
reds of love.

I know skies
I know currents
the dawn aroused
and I've seen what men

burst by lightning
waterspouts, night
like a flock of doves
believe they have seen.

I've seen the sun
with long clotted solidiments
like actors in
rolling waves faraway

low and lit and violet
splotched by mystic horrors;
an ancient play
shiver like a compass.

I've dreamed of green nights
and kisses rising slow
the circulation of
and the yellow-blue awakenings

with sparkling snow
to the eyes of the sea
resins unknown
of phosphorescent harmony.

For many months
beating the reefs
never even dreaming
of Virgins could appease

I followed the swells
like hysterical cattle
how the luminous feet
the snorting snouts of the Sea.

I've slammed myself
mixing petals
eyes and human skin
rainbows reined

into Floridas incredible
with panther
while under oceanic skies
the sea-green herds.

I've seen vast marshes festering
with entire Leviathans
as water crashed down
the horizon cataracting

and fishtraps packed
rotting in the reeds
upon the calm
into the abyss;

and pearly seas and glacial waves
and hideous wrecks
where giant insect-
flop off twisted trees

and silver suns and skies ablaze
in the darkest depths
eaten serpents
wafting black perfumes.

From the deep blue
those singing fish of gold
flowery foam
and wordless winds

I would have rather shown
to children though
rocked my hold
have given me wings.

Weary with poles and zones
a sobbing martyr swaying me
flowers to me
while I remained

the sea would sometimes be
and raising her shadowy
full of little yellow cups
like a woman on my knees.

A virtual island
I sailed along
of mockingbirds
tied to my lines

tossing side to side
in the squabble and squirt
as drowned men sank
backwards into sleep.

But for me, lost boat
hurricane-hurled
no merchant marine
fished my drunken

in the mane of the cove
in the ether of no birds
or battleship could have
corpse from the sea:

being free, and ascending
as if breaching the wall
bearing fantastic jam
those lichens of sun)

smoking in a violet fog
of the reddening sky
(those sky-blue boogers
to the fancy poets up above.

from absinthe to abyssinia

Speckled with electric crescents I ran
the mad plank led by ebony seahorses
as summers bludgeoned the ultramarine
smashing the skies with funnels ablaze.

Trembling I felt the groan at fifty leagues
of Behemoths in heat and Maelstroms thick;
eternal spinner of blue motionless
I yearn for the ancient parapets of Europe.

I have seen the constellated seas where islands reveal
heavens in delirium to galleyslaves rowing:
Oh Vigor of a million golden birds to come
Do you banish yourself to sleep in these bottomless nights?

I have cried excessively each Dawn is full of grief
all moons are atrocious every sun bitter:
a sour love has swollen me with intoxicated lethargy
I wish my keel would burst and the sea would take me.

But if I yearn for the waters of Europe
it's for the cool dark pool where a sad squatting boy
releases like a butterfly a delicate boat
toward the twilight's perfume.

So no longer can I bathe in your languor, oh waves
nor follow in the wake of cottonships
nor endure the pride of oriflamme and flag
as I drift beneath the prisonship eyes

of Atrocity!

Wastelands of Love[18]

PREFACE

These are the writings of a young man, a very young man, who could have grown up anywhere; without mother or country, indifferent to every- thing, fleeing all morals, just like several pathetic young men before him. But bored and confused, he only led himself toward death, as if heading for a hor- rible fatal modesty. Having never loved women — though passionate! — his heart and soul and strength increased with every strange sad accident. So he dreamed of his loves who came to him in the streets and in his bed. And from what befell them, sweet religious reflections arose, recalling perhaps, the con- tinuous slumber of bold but circumcised Muslims! This bizarre suffering, however, holds a troubling truth: there's a sincere desire that this Soul lost among us, who apparently aspires to death, find in his last moment some grave consolations, and be worthy of his doom!

I

—

Definitely, it was the same terrain. The same rustic house of my youth: the same room with the same faded pastoral scenes of lions and weapons over the door. In the dining room there were wines, candles, antique panels. The table was large. And the maids! There were a few as I recall. An old friend of mine was there, a young priest dressed in robes to be more free. I remember his purple room with yellow-papered windowpanes, and his hidden books soaked by the sea!

I was left alone in that endless farmhouse, reading in the kitchen, drying my muddy clothes before the visitors with their drawing-room chatter — scared to death by the murmurs of the morning milk and the night of the last century.

I was in a very dark room — what was I doing? A servant girl was coming my way — she was just a little pup, but to me she was beautiful, with an indescribable maternal nobility: pure and familiar, incredibly bewitching! She pinched my arm.

I can't remember her face very well — nor her arm and its flesh I squeezed, nor her mouth I seized. Like a small desperate wave, her tongue kept probing ceaselessly — for something. I threw her down in the darkness of the corner, in a basket of padding and sails. I only remember that her panties had white lace.

Then, oh despair! The walls blurred into the shadows of the trees as I sank into the amorous sadness of the night.

This time I saw Woman — in the City — whom I spoke with. But now she speaks to me.

I was in a bedroom. Without light. Someone came to tell me she had arrived — and then I saw her in my bed, all mine. Without light! And this thrilled me, because this was the family home. Distress gripped me! I was in rags, and she, a woman of the world, was giving herself to me. She had to go! The unspeakable agony: I took her, then let her fall from the bed, practically naked, and being indescribably weak, I fell upon her and we drug through the rugs. Without light! Room by room, the house began to glow in red. Then she disappeared, and I shed more tears than God would've wanted.

I went out and into the endless city. Oh weariness! Drowned in the deafness of the night and the flight away from happiness. It was snowing like a winter night trying to smother the world forever. My friends, to whom I cried "Where is she?" replied in lies. I stood before the windows where she goes every night — I was running through a buried garden. I had been rejected. I cried incredibly. And finally, I descended to a place of dust, and sitting on a skeletal heap, I let loose the tears of my body — though exhaustion, as always, returned to me.

I realized that She had an everyday life, that a star would sooner be formed than happiness ever happen to me. She has not returned and will never return, that Goddess who came to me, unexpectedly. Truly, I cried this time more than all the children in the world.

Rough Drafts[19]

Several in Samaria had shown their faith in him, though he had never seen them. Arrogant Samaria, affluent and false-hearted, was an egotist more strict in its observance of Protestant law than Judah was of the Ten Commandments. Universal wealth was permitted there, but little enlightened discussion. A sophisticated slave and soldier to routine, several prophets had been slaughtered there after being praised.

A woman at a well spoke forbodingly to Jesus: "You are a prophet, you know what I have done."

Men and women once believed in prophets. Now they believe in politicians.

Not far from this strange city, unable to physically threaten it, Jesus wondered what would happen if he appeared fantastically before them, and what he would do if they took him for a prophet.

But Jesus had nothing to say to Samaria.

In the thin bewitching oxygen, the inhabitants of Galilee welcomed him with curious cheer: they had seen him shaken by holy rage, whipping the livestock merchants and money-changers from the temple, and they thought this was the miracle of a pale and furious youth.

Jesus felt his hand in a heavy hand of rings, and then against the lips of an official on his knees in the dust. And his half-bald head was pleasing to Jesus.

The carts sped through the narrow streets, moving swiftly for such a small town. Then everything seemed too calm.

Jesus drew back his hand with the haughty gesture of a little girl: "You will not believe in miracles unless you see them happen."

Jesus had not performed any yet. In a pink and green dining room at a wedding, he spoke sharply to the Virgin. Yet no one in Capernaum, in the marketplace or on the quays, spoke of the wine of Cana. Except, perhaps, the merchant class.

Jesus said: "Go, your son will live" and the official went away as if he were drugged, and Jesus kept on going, following the roads less traveled, where heliotrope and morning glories were magically glowing. And finally in the distance he saw the dusty plains, with buttercups and daisies crying in the light of day.

Bethzatha, the pool of five porticoes, was a place of ennui. It looked like a depraved washhouse, always moldy and heavy with rain, with beggars loitering on the stairway, pale in the gloaming of storms foreshadowing the lightning of hell. They joked about their blue-blind eyes, their clean white sheets, and the blue ones wrapped around their stubs. Oh military laundry house, oh filthy public bath! The water was always black. Even the cripples never fell in — not even in their dreams.

It was there that Jesus first took action with the slovenly cripples. It was a day in February, or March, or April, when the afternoon sun was making a great sickle of light stretch across the gravely darkened water, while far beyond the invalids, it was possible to see each ray awakening the crystals and buds and poetry — shining whitely like an angel asleep on its side, as infinite reflections rippled.

Those with more sensitive souls (their sins being young tough sons of the demon, who had made these men more horrible than monsters) were driven to jump into the water. Then the cripples went in, no longer laughing, but longing.

The first ones, it was said, would come out healed. But no. On the steps their sins forced them back and sent them seeking other places — for their Demon could only remain where alms were certain.

Jesus entered soon after noon. Nobody washed nor led their oxen to water. The light in the pool was yellow like the last leaves on the vine. The divine Master Demon was leaning against a pillar, watching with the sons of Sin, before joining them in sticking out his tongue and laughing at Jesus.

Then the Paralytic, who was lying on his side, arose and walked with confidence across the portico, before disappearing into the city — as the Damned looked on.

Sketches of Season in Hell[20]

BAD BLOOD

Yes, I have a vice that starts and stops again. With my open breast exposed, I can see a horribly crippled heart inside. In childhood I knew its roots of suffering in my side: but today it rises toward the sky, it is much stronger than I, it beats me, drags me, hurls me to the ground.

I hear that I should deny my pleasure, avoid duty and not bring my diminishing innocence, elitist treason, timidness and disgust to the world.

Let's go! The desert, the burden, the violence, misfortune, the anger and ennui — The delirium of my fears will surely disappear in Hell.

What demon should I praise? What beast should I pay homage to? What blood should flow through my veins? What screams should I scream? Which lie should I tell? What Holy image should I destroy? Which hearts should I break?

I should avoid the stupid hand of justice and death instead. I will hear its sad ballad sung in the markets of the past.

Hard life, pure brutalness. And then to lift the coffin lid with a withered fist, to sit there and choke. I will not grow old from old age! There is no danger, terror is not French.

Ah! I am so alone that I am offering my drive for perfection to anything that appears divine. Another hideous deal.

Oh my abnegation, my inconceivable charity. *De Profundis Domine!* Am I so stupid?

Enough. This is punishment! No more talk of innocence. Let's move on. Oh! My loins are being ripped from me, my heart is groaning, my breast is burning, my head is thumping in the sun while night rolls in my eyes.

Where are we going? To battle?

Ah! My soul, my filthy youth. Go!... go, others are advancing... with tools, with weapons.

Oh! Oh! I am weakness and stupidity!

Let's go! Fire upon me. Or I will surrender! Wounded, I hurl myself flat on my belly, where horses trample me!

Ah!

I'll get used to it.

And I'll live the French life, holding to the Path of Honor.

FALSE CONVERSION

Oh unfortunate day! I swallowed an exquisite mouthful of poison. The rage of despair makes me hate nature, everything, and myself, which I'd like to rip apart. I'm thrice blessed by the advice given me. My entrails burn, the violence of the venom twists my limbs, deforming them. I am dying of thirst. I am choking. I cannot scream. It's hell, an eternity of pain. The fire rises. Come on demon, come on devil, come on Satan, stir up the flames. I am burning like I should — it's a fine and beautiful hell.

I envisioned the conversion, the good, the happiness, the health. I can describe the vision — no one can be a poet in hell.

It was an apparition of thousands of entrancing nymphs, a commendable concert, a spiritual of strength and peace, noble ambitions and who knows what else!

Ah: Noble ambitions! My hatred. I commence again my enraged existence with anger in my blood, a bestial life, stupidity, my misfortune and that of others — which hardly matters to me, but that's life! If damnation is eternal. Still, that's life. Has the execution of religious laws sown a similar faith in my spirit? My parents created my misfortune and their own, which also hardly matters to me. They abused my innocence. Oh! The idea of baptism. People have lived badly, as people do now, and there are those who don't feel anything at all! My baptism and weakness enslaves me. But again, that's life.

from absinthe to abyssinia

Later on, the delights of damnation will be more profound. I recognize damnation well. A man who wants to mutilate himself is surely damned! I believe that I am in hell, therefore I am. Quick, give me a crime. May I tumble into nothingness, through the law of man.

Shut up. Shut up! Shame and reproach are by my side. Satan told me his fire is stupid and vile, and that my anger is ghastly. Enough. Shut up! These are mistakes whispered in my ear: magic, alchemy, mysticism, false perfumes, naïve tunes. Satan is in charge of this. This is why poets are damned. No, that's not it.

I can't believe I hold the truth. That I have a sound and set judgement and am entirely ready for perfection. And now, pride! I am just a wooden character with withering skin upon my head. Oh God! My God! My God! I am afraid, have mercy on me! Ah! I'm thirsty. Oh my childhood, my village, the meadows, the lake, the beach, the moonlight when the bell tolled twelve and Satan laughed from the belltower. — I'm getting stupid! Oh Mary, Holy Virgin, false sentiment, false prayer.

Excerpts from Season in Hell

Once, if I remember correctly, my life was a feast where every heart opened and all wines flowed.

One night, I sat Beauty on my knee — and I found her bitter, so insulted her.

I armed myself against justice.

I fled. Oh witches, oh misery, oh hatred, I entrusted my treasure to you!

I was able to make all human hope in my spirit disappear. I pounced silently like a ferocious beast in order to strangle all joy.

Perishing, I called to the executioners, begging to bite their rifle butts. I called to the scourge to smother me with sand and blood. Misfortune was my god. I stretched myself out in the mud. I dried myself in the air of crime. And I played some pretty good tricks on madness.

Then spring brought the horrid laughter of the idiot to me.

But recently, having found myself on the verge of squawking my last *squawk*, I dreamed of seeking the key to the ancient feast where I could feed my faith again.

from absinthe to abyssinia

Charity is this key — an inspiration that proves I have dreamed!

"You will always be a hyena, etc!..." screamed the demon, crowning me with poppies. "Die from all your appetites, your ego, and all your deadly sins!"

Ah! I've had enough: — But, dear Satan, I beg of you, regard me with a less incensed eye! And in awaiting a few belated and cowardly acts, I will tear out for you — who likes writing that's not descriptive and didactic — these hideous pages from my notes of the damned.

BAD BLOOD

From my Gaulish ancestors, I inherited their blue-white eyes, their narrow skulls and awkwardness in fighting. And my clothing is just as barbaric as theirs. But at least I don't go buttering my hair.

The Gauls were the worst beast-skinners and field-burners of their time.

From them I possess: a love for idols and blasphemy — oh! all the vices: anger, lust — magnificent lust! — but above all, sloth and deceit.

I am horrified by all trades. All bosses and workers are wretched peasants. A plume in the hand isn't worth more than a plow in the hand — What a century of hands! — And my hands will never be mine. Or else I'd be domestic. The honesty of beggary cuts me to the core. Criminals are just as disgusting as eunuchs: but I am intact and not bothered by that.

Who made my tongue so treacherous that it guided and guarded my laziness until now!? Without using my body to get by, more idle than a toad, I have lived everywhere — There's no family in Europe I don't know. Like mine, they cling with their lives to the Declaration of Human Rights — I have known every one of their sons!

from absinthe to abyssinia

If only I had some predecessors somewhere in the history of France!

But no, nothing.

It's quite evident to me that I have always been of an inferior race. I cannot understand revolt. My race has never rebelled except to pillage: like wolves with beasts they didn't kill.

I remember the history of France, eldest daughter of the Church. As a simple villager I'd wander across the holy land; my mind knows roads of the Swabian plains, visions of Byzantium, ramparts of Jerusalem: the Cult of Mary and the compassion of the crucified awake in me amidst a thousand magical blasphemies. Like a leper I sat upon pottery shards and nettles under walls eroded by the sun. Later, as a warrior, I slept outside in the Aryan night.

Ah! There's more: In red glades I've danced in black masses with old women and children.

But I can't remember farther back than Christianity and this land. I will never stop seeing myself in that past. Though always, alone: no family — and what language did I even speak? I never asked Christ for advice, nor those lords who represent him.

What I was last century: I only find myself today. No more vague wars or vagabonds. People are the inferior race and they have enveloped the world, along with reason, nationalism and science.

Oh! Science! Everything has been defined. For the body: the last sacrament! For the soul: medicine, philosophy: homemade remedies, popular songs. And the royal games which princes forbade, yet played! Geography, cosmography, mechanics, chemistry!...

Science, the new nobility! Progress! The world keeps spinning! Why wouldn't it?

It's the vision of numbers. We're moving toward the *Spirit*. It's imminent. What I say is prophecy. I know. And I don't know — how to explain myself without pagan words. I wish I would just shut up.

Vi(o)lations[21]

Ancient animals were squirting
their cocks greased
Our fathers displayed
by the folds of their sheaths

even on the run
in excrement and blood.
their members proudly
and the grain of their balls.

For the female of the Middle Ages
a solid cockswain
Even Kleber
apparently had

be she angel or swine
was always in mind;
with his slightly lying pants
the goods it took.

Furthermore, man
but the enormity of his member
A sterile time has struck:

is the proudest mammal
is amazingly misleading.
the horse and ox

have bridled their desire
to display their genital
in the shrubs of swarming

and nobody dares
pride anymore
children at play.

Ass Sonnet

Our asses are not like theirs.
unbuttoned men
or shamelessly bathing
I have seen the shape

I have frequently seen
behind hedges
where children stray.
and fate of man's ass.

Firmer and paler than theirs
with obvious planes
but for women
blooms only in that

ours is supplied
veiling the hairy mesh;
their long bushy satin
enchanting crack.

It's a marvelous moving
as in carvings
in tables

ingeniousness
of angels
with cheeky hollow smiles.

Oh! If only I were naked
my forehead before
then we'd be free

seeking pleasure, seeking peace
his glorious length
to murmur and weep!

ASSHOLE SONNET

Dark and puckered
humbly hidden in the moss
as love flows
to the crater's rim

like a lavender carnation
it breathes, damp
down the soft ramp
of his pale ass.

Filaments
have cried beneath cruel winds
across small clots
to lose themselves

with milky tears
shoving them
of reddish loam
in the beckoning slope.

My dreams have joined
physical coitus
browning his nest

my soul of jealous
to his puckery duct
with sobs.

It's the swooning sack
the tube the heavenly
in the womanly wet

and the dancing dick
seed descends
of paradise.

from absinthe to abyssinia

Bottom

Reality being too thorny for my grand character, I found myself nevertheless with my lady, a great gray-blue bird rising toward the mouldings and trailing my wings in the shadows of the evening.

I was, at the foot of her bed, supporting her beloved jewels and physical artistry, a great hoary bear with bruised violet gums, my eyes on the silver and crystal of the cabinets.

Then everything blurred bright aquamarine.

In the morning — a querulous June dawn — I ran into the fields an ass, brandishing my grief and howling to the Sabine women of the suburbs who came to throw themselves on my chest.

We are hungry in the barracks
    It's true...

Emanations, explosions. A genie:
    "I am gruyère!"
Lefebvre: "Keller!"
The genie: "I am Brie!"
The soldiers cut their bread:
    "That's life!"
The génie: "I am Roquefort!"
    "This'll be our death!..."
    "I am gruyère!"
    And Brie... etc.

Waltz

We've been joined together, Lefebvre and me, etc.

PART II

LETTERS, REPORTS, WORKS
FROM AFRICA AND AFTER

Fragment from a Letter to Verlaine[23]

Charleville, April 1872

... My work is farther away from me than my fingernail is from my eye. It's shit for me! Shit for me! Shit for me? Shit for me! Shit for me! Shit!

. . . .

When you see me eat shit, only then will you know that I am not expensive to feed!...

Rimbaud

Rimbaud's Statement to the Police[24]

(July 10, 1873
around 8 o'clock in the evening)

For a year, I have been living in London with a Monsieur Verlaine. We were newspaper correspondents and we gave French lessons. He had become impossible to get along with and I had expressed my desire to return to Paris.

Four days ago he left me to go to Brussels. He then sent me a telegram asking that I come join him. I have been here for two days, lodging with him and his mother at 1 Rue des Brasseurs, where I kept expressing my desire to return to Paris. He responded:

"Go ahead, leave and see what happens!"

That morning, he bought a revolver in the Passage des Galeries St. Hubert, which he showed me upon his return around noon. We then went to the Grand Place at the Hotel des Brasseurs where we continued to chat about my departure. Going back to the lodging around two o'clock, he locked the door and sat down in front of it. He then loaded his revolver, fired two shots and said:

"This'll teach you to want to leave!"

from absinthe to abyssinia

These gunshots were fired from three meters away. The first wounded me in the left wrist, the second missed. His mother was present and gave me first aid. I then went to St. Jean's Hospital where I was bandaged. I was accompanied by Verlaine and his mother. The three of us then returned to the house. Verlaine kept telling me not to leave him and to stay with him, but I didn't wish to consent and left around seven in the evening, accompanied by Verlaine and his mother. When we arrived in the vicinity of Place Rouppe, Verlaine took a few steps forward, then came back toward me. I saw him put his hand in his pocket to grab his revolver, so I turned and retraced my steps. I met a police officer and told him what happened to me, and he invited Verlaine to follow him to the police station.

If the latter would have allowed me to leave freely, I wouldn't have lodged my complaint about the wound he gave me.

A. Rimbaud

Verlaine's Statement to the Police

July 10, 1873

I arrived in Brussels four days ago, miserable and desperate. I have known Rimbaud for more than a year. I lived with him in London, which I left four days ago to come live in Brussels, to be closer to my affairs, as I plead a case for separation with my wife who lives in Paris and pretends that I am having immoral relations with Rimbaud.

I wrote my wife that if she didn't come join me within three days, I would blow my brains out, which is why I bought the revolver this morning in the Passage des Galeries St. Hubert, with the holster and a box of bullets, for the sum of 23 francs.

After my arrival in Brussels, I received a letter from Rimbaud asking if he could join me. I sent him a telegram saying that I would wait for him, and he arrived two days ago. Today, seeing me so miserable, he wanted to leave me. I gave in to a moment of madness and shot at him. He lodged no complaint at that time. My mother and I took him to St. Jean's Hospital to get bandaged, and then we returned together. Rimbaud was in a rush to leave. My mother gave him 20 francs for his trip and on the way to the train station he pretended that I wanted to kill him.

P. Verlaine

from absinthe to abyssinia

Bremen the 14 mai 77

The untersigned Arthur Rimbaud — Born in Charleville (France) — Aged 23 — 5 ft. 6 height — Good healthy, — Late a teacher of sciences and languages — Recently deserted from the 47e Regiment of the French army, — Actually in Bremen without any means, the French Consul refusing any Relief.

Would like to know on which conditions he could conclude an immediate engagement in the American navy.

Speaks and writes English, German, French, Italian and Spanish.

Has been four months as a sailor in a Scotch bark, from Java to Queenstown, from August to December 76.

Would be very honoured and grateful to receive an answer.

John Arthur Rimbaud

Report on the Ogaden[26]

by Monsieur Arthur Rimbaud
Agent of Monsieurs Mazeran, Viannay and Bardey,
in Harar (East Africa)

Here is the information reported from our first expedition into the Ogaden.

Ogaden is the name of a group of tribes of Somali origin and of the region they occupy, generally delineated on the maps between the Somali tribes of the Habr-Gerhadjis, the Doulbohantes, the Midgertines, and the Hawïa to the north, the east and the south. To the west, the borders of the Ogadin are adjacent to the Gallas (pastoral Ennyan tribes), all the way to the Wabi River, which separates them from the great Oromo tribe of the Oroussis.

There are two roads from Harar to the Ogaden: one is east of the city, towards Boursouque, and to the south of Mount Condoudo through War-Ali with three trading stations on the way to the borders of the Ogaden. This is the route that our agent M. Sotiro took. The distance from Harar to the point where he stopped in Rar Hersi is equal to the distance from Harar to Biocabouba on the road to Zeila, about 140 kilometers. This road is the least dangerous of the two and it has water.

The other road goes to the southeast from Harar by way of the Hérer River Crossing, the market in Babili, Wara-Heban and the plundering Somali-Galla tribes of Hawïa.

The name "Hawïa" seems to specifically designate tribes formed through a mixture of Gallas and Somalis, of which a fraction exists in the northwest beneath the plateau of Harar. A second fraction exists to the south of Harar on the road to the Ogaden, and finally, a third very large fraction is southeast of the Ogaden, towards Sahel. The three fractions exist completely independent of each other.

Like all the surrounding Somali tribes, the Ogadins are entirely nomadic and their region completely lacks roads or markets. Even from the exterior, there are no specific roads leading to this area. The roads drawn on the maps, from the Ogaden to Berberah, or Mogdischo or Broua, probably simply indicate the general direction of traffic.

The Ogaden is a plateau of almost flat steppes, generally sloping to the southeast: its height is presumably half of that of the mountains of Harar (1800 meters).

Its climate is therefore hotter than Harar's. It seems to have two rainy seasons: one in October and the other in March when the rains are frequent, but light.

The waterways in the Ogaden are not significant. We have counted four descending from the mountains of Harar: one, the Fafan, finds its source in the Condoudo and descends through Boursouque, turns in the Ogaden, and plunges into the Wabi at a point named Faf, half-way to Mogdischo; it is the largest waterway in the Ogaden. The Hérer is a little river also coming from the Garo Condoudo, then skirting Babili. Four days south of Harar, coming down from Alas, the Hérer meets the Ennya, the Gobeli, and the Moyo, then flows into the Wabi in the Ogaden in Nokob. The other small river is the Dokhta, starting in Warra Heban and descending to the Wabi, probably in the direction of the Hérer.

In Ogaden Major, heavy rains in the mountains of Harar

and Boursouque cause temporary torrents and light floods which, when they occur, call the tribes in that direction. In dry times, on the other hand, there is a general movement to return to the Wabi.

The general appearance of the Ogaden is of tall grass steppes full of stony lacunas. The trees, at least in the parts explored by our explorers, are those of the Somali deserts: mimosa, gum, etc. Near the Wabi, however, the population is sedentary and agrarian. They cultivate sorghum almost exclusively and even employ slaves from Aroussis and other Galla tribes beyond the river. One fraction of the Malingour tribe in Ogaden Major also plants sorghum, and there are some villages of Cheikhache farmers here and there as well.

Like all the people of these regions, the Ogadins are constantly at war with their neighbors and among themselves.

The Ogadins hold to the old traditions of their ancestors. We have consistently heard that they are descended from Rar Abdallah and Rar Ishay ("Rar" signifies children, the family and the home; in the language of Galla they say "Warra"). Rar Abdallah was the descendant of Rar Hersi and Rar Hammadèn; these are the two main families of Ogaden Major.

Rar Ishay engendered Rar Ali and Rar Aroun. The rars are subdivided into numerous secondary families. These tribes were visited by M. Sotiro. They are descended from Rar Hersi and are called the Malingours, the Aïl, the Oughas, the Sementars and the Magan.

The Ogadins are divided according to their head chiefs, known as "oughazes." The Oughaz of Malingour, our friend Omar Hussein, is the most powerful in Ogaden Major, and he appears to have authority over all tribes between Habr Gerhadji and the Wabi. His father came to Harar during the days of Pasha Raof, who gave gifts of weapons and clothing to him.

As for Omar Hussein, he has never left his tribes, where he is renowned as a warrior and is content with respecting the authority of Egypt from afar.

Moreover, the Egyptians seem to regard the Ogadins, as well as the Somalis and Danakils, as their subjects, or rather, their natural allies as Muslims, who would never entertain the thought of invading their territories.

The Ogadins, at least those we have seen, are tall and generally more red than black. They keep their heads bare and their hair short, dress themselves with comparatively clean clothing, and wear sandals. They carry ritual prayer rugs on their shoulders, sabers and purification gourds on their hips, walking sticks in their hands, and both a small spear and a big spear.

Their daily business is squatting in groups beneath trees some distance from the camp, and weapons in hand, deliberating indefinitely on various issues. Beyond these meetings, and riding around looking for water and neighbors to raid, they are completely inactive. The women and children take care of the livestock, decorate the huts, load the caravans and manufacture utensils, including milk jugs like those in Somaliland and mats for camels that convert into the houses of migrant villages when raised on sticks.

Some blacksmiths wander through the tribes and fashion iron for daggers and spears.

The Ogadins are not aware of any minerals in their midst.

They are Muslim fanatics. Each camp has its priest who chants prayers at appointed hours. There are "wodads" (scholars) in each tribe; they know the Koran, how to write in Arabic, and are also improvisational poets.

Ogadin families are large in number. M. Sotiro's guide had 60 sons and grandsons. When the wife of an Ogadin man gives birth, the latter abstains from all commerce with her until the child is capable of walking alone. Naturally, the husband marries one or several others in the interim, but always with the same understanding.

Their herds consist of zebu, short-haired sheep, goats, mongrel horses, milk camels, and ostriches, of which the rearing is a custom among all Ogadins. Each village possesses a few dozen ostriches grazing nearby, under the watchful eye of the children. Ostriches even lie by the fire in the huts. Both males and females are shackled on their thighs and follow the caravans behind the camels, which they are almost as tall as.

Ostriches are plumed three or four times per year; almost half a pound of black feathers, and about 60 white feathers, are plucked from each. Ostrich owners hold these feathers as extremely valuable.

There are many wild ostriches. The bow-hunters, covered in female ostrich hides, shoot the males when they approach.

The dead feathers are of less value than the live feathers. Domestic ostriches are captured at a young age, but the Ogadins do not let them reproduce.

In central Ogaden, elephants are not large in number or size. They are hunted on the Fafan, but the place where they are most legion, and go to die, is the shore of the Wabi. They are hunted there by farmers on the river (known as Dones) who are a Somali mix of Galla and Swahili. They hunt on foot and kill their prey with enormous spears. The Ogadins hunt on horseback: as a group of fifteen or so horsemen distract the elephant in front of it and along its flanks, an experienced hunter chops away at its shins from behind with a saber.

They also use poisoned arrows. This poison, called "ouabay," and used in all of Somaliland, is made from the ground, boiled roots of a shrub. We are sending you a piece. According to the Somalis, the soil around these shrubs is always covered with snake skins, and all the surrounding shrubs are withered. Furthermore, this poison works slowly. Hence, natives wounded by these arrows (also used for war) cut off the afflicted part and remain safe.

Ferocious beasts are rare in the Ogaden. The natives, however, speak of snakes, including a horned species with deadly breath. The most common wild animals are gazelles, antelopes, giraffes and rhinoceroses, of which the skin is used to make shields. The Wabi has all the animals of the great rivers: elephants, crocodiles, hippopotami, etc.

A race regarded as inferior exists among the Ogaden and their numbers are quite high: the Mitganes, who appear to belong to a Somali race that speaks the same language. They only marry among themselves, and occupy themselves primarily with hunting elephants, ostriches, etc.

The Mitganes are distributed between the tribes, and in times of war are utilized as spies and allies. The Ogadins eat elephant, camel and ostrich, and the Mitganes eat donkey and animals found dead, which is considered a sin.

The Mitganes even have some highly populated villages among the Danakils of Haouache, where they are renowned as hunters.

A political custom, and an Ogadin feast, occurs when tribes of a certain area meet each year on a set date.

Justice is rendered within families and generally by the oughazes.

In the history of mankind, no one has ever seen such an incredible amount of merchandise from the Ogaden as what we obtained there for a few hundred thalers. The little that we do bring back from there, however, comes to us at quite a price, since merchandise must be used as gifts for our guides and hosts along all roads. The Oughaz has personally received a few hundred dollars worth of gold cord from us, as well as muslin, and gifts of all kinds, which are associated with us appreciatively. This is the good that has resulted from the expedition. M. Sotiro is to be congratulated for the wisdom and diplomacy he has shown in this case. Whereas our competitors have been hounded, cursed, beaten and murdered, and have been, due to their own disasters, the cause of terrible wars between tribes, we have established ourselves as allies of the Oughaz and have made ourselves known in all of Rar Hersi.

Omar Hussein wrote to us in Harar and is waiting for us to go down with him and his Arabs, all the way to the Wabi, only a few days away from our first trading station.

This is actually our goal. One of us, or some ambitious native on our behalf, could gather a ton of ivory in a few weeks, to export directly through a franchise in Berbera. Natives from Habr-Awal, who go down on the Wabi with a few sodas and some unbleached cotton on their shoulders, return to Boulhar with hundreds of dollars of feathers. A few donkeys loaded with ten or so lengths of fabric have brought back fifteen loads of ivory.

We have therefore decided to create a trading post on the Wabi River near a point called Eimeh, a large permanent village situated on the Ogaden side of the river, just eight days from Harar by caravan.

Letter to His Mother and Sister

Harar, December 21, 1883

I am still doing well and I hope you are doing the same.

On this occasion, I wish you a happy new year for 1884.

Nothing new here.

All my best,

Rimbaud

To the Bosphore Égyptien[27]

Cairo, August 1887

Monsieur,

Having returned from a journey in Abyssinia and Harar, I would like to call your attention to the following notes on the actual state of things in that region. I believe they will contain some previously unpublished information. As for the opinions noted here, they come from my seven years of living in the region.

Since this is about a round-trip journey between Obock, Shoa, Harar and Zeila, allow me to explain that I went down to Tadjoura at the beginning of last year with the goal of forming a caravan to Shoa there.

My caravan was made up of a few thousand percussion rifles and an order for tools and various supplies for King Ménélik. It was held up for an entire year in Tadjoura by the Danakils, who deal with all travelers by opening their road only after having stolen everything they can from them. Another caravan, which disembarked from Tadjoura with some of my merchandise, took fifteen months to get underway. One thousand Remington rifles brought by the late Soleillet at the same time are still down there, after nineteen months, beneath the only grove of palm trees in the village.

About 60 kilometers from Tadjoura, with just six quick stops along the way, the caravans descend to the Salted Lake on horrible roads, like lunar landscapes we can only imagine. It seems that a French company was actually formed for the exploitation of this salt.

Salt does exist on these vast flats and is probably quite deep, but no one has ever measured its depth. Analysis would declare it chemically pure, even though it is found deposited without filtration on the shores of the lake. Still, it is strongly doubted that the sale of salt would cover the expenses for the building of a road for the establishment of a Decauville between this beach and that of the Gulf of Goubbet-Kérab. The expenses for personnel and labor would be excessively high and workers would have to be imported because Danakil Bedouins do not work. And then there would be the maintenance of armed troops to protect the work.

To return to the question of commercial outlets, it should be noted that the saline of Sheik Othman, produced near Aden by an Italian company under exceptionally advantageous conditions, has apparently not yet found a market. Mountains of salt are still in stock.

The Ministry of the Navy has granted this concession to the petitioners who have conducted trade in Shoa in the past, on condition that they procure the agreement of the interested chiefs on the coast and in the interior. The government has put a tax on every ton and has a fixed rate on unlimited exploitation by the natives. The interested chiefs are: the Sultan of Tadjoura, who would be the hereditary proprietor of a few mountains of rubble near the lake (he is quite disposed to sell his rights); the Chief of the Debné tribes, who is on our road from the lake to Hérer; Sultan Loïta, who earns a monthly payment of 150 thalers from the government for bothering travelers as little as possible; Sultan Hanfaré of Alussa, who can find salt anywhere, but pretends to have the right everywhere among the Danakils; and finally Ménélik, who the Debnés and others annually bring thousands of camels to for thousands of tons of salt. Ménélik has made demands upon the government after being warned about the way the company works and learning of the gift of the concession. But the part reserved in the concession is sufficient for the business of the Debné tribe and for the culinary needs of Shoa, since grains of salt do not pass as money in Abyssinia.

Our road is called the Gobât Road, from the name of its fifteenth trading station where our allies the Debnés usually graze their herds. They are about 23 stops from Hérer, through the most terrifying territory this side of Africa, which is highly dangerous due to the fact that the Debnés, the most wretched foreign tribes using the road for transport, are eternally at war with the Moudeïto and Assa-Imara tribes on one hand, and with the Issa Somalis on the other.

In Hérer, the Danakils and the Issas generally graze their herds without any land disputes in pastures at an altitude of around 800 meters, at about 60 kilometers from the foot of the plateau of the Galla Itous.

From Hérer, one can get to the Hawash River in eight or nine days. Ménélik has decided to establish an armed post on the plains of Hérer for the protection of the caravans; this post would be linked to those of the Abyssinians in the Itous Mountains.

On the road from Hérer, Dedjatch Mékonène, representing the King in Harar, has shipped from Harar to Shoa 3,000,000 rounds of ammunition and other munitions that the English commissaries abandoned so Emir Abdoullahi would profit during the Egyptian evacuation.

This whole road was impressively constructed for the first time by M. Jules Borelli on his recent trip to Harar in May 1886. It is geodesically connected to the topography and is parallel to the Itous Mountains.

Arriving at the Hawash, one is stupefied to think back on the canal-digging plans of certain explorers. Poor Soleillet had a special boat built in Nantes for this purpose. The Hawash is a small winding channel obstructed every step of the way by trees and rocks. I have crossed it at several points hundreds of kilometers apart and it is absolutely impossible to descend, even during floods. Furthermore, it is bordered on all sides by forests and deserts, far from the commercial centers, and it never branches off with any road. Ménélik had two bridges built on the Hawash; one on the road from Entotto to Gouragné, the other on the road from Ankober to Harar, made by the Itous. These simple foot-bridges are built from tree trunks and are meant for the passage of troops during the rains and floods. They are remarkable works for Shoa.

Upon arriving in Shoa, all expenses paid, the transport of 100 camel-loads of my merchandise cost me 8000 thalers; that's 80 thalers per camel for a distance of only 500 kilometers. This proportion is not consistent with any of the other African-caravan roads, yet I traveled with the utmost economy and a lot of experience in these regions. In all respects, this road is disastrous and has unfortunately been replaced by the road from Zeila to Harar and from Harar to Shoa, built by the Itous.

Ménélik was still in the Harar area when I reached Farri, the point of arrival and departure for the caravans, and the outer limits of the Danakil race. News soon arrived in Ankober of the victory of the King and his entry into Harar, along with the announcement of his return, which took about twenty days. He entered Entotto preceded by musicians blasting Egyptian trumpets obtained in Harar, and his troops and booty followed with two Krupp cannons hauled by 80 men each.

For a long time Ménélik has been intending on capturing Harar, where he believed a formidable arsenal to be, so warned French and English political representatives on the coast. In the last few years, the Abyssinian troops established there have been regularly ransoming the Itous. Also, ever since the departure of Pasha Radouan with the Egyptian troops, Emir Abdullaï has been organizing a small army and has been dreaming of becoming the Mahdi of the Muslim tribes in central Harar. He wrote to Ménélik claiming the Hawash frontier and advised him to convert to Islam. When an Abyssinian trading post was set up a few days away from Harar, the Emir sent a few cannons and some Turcs who were still in his service to disperse the Abyssinians. The latter were beaten, so Ménélik, irritated, went by foot from Entotto with about 30,000 warriors. The meeting took place in Salanko, 60 kilometers west of Harar, where Pasha Nadi beat the Galla tribes of the Méta and the Oborra four years before.

The engagement scarcely lasted a quarter of an hour. The Emir only had a few hundred Remingtons and the rest of his troops fought with no weapons at all. Three thousand warriors were cut up with sabers and crushed in a blink of an eye by the King of Shoa. Nearly 200 Sudanese, Egyptians and Turcs left with Abdullaï after the Egyptian evacuation and perished with the Galla and Somali warriors. This is why it is said that when the Shoan soldiers (who have never killed any whites) returned, they brought back the testicles of all foreigners in Harar.

The Emir was able to flee to Harar, then left the very same night to seek refuge with the Chief of the Guerry tribe to the east of Harar in the direction of Berbera. Ménélik arrived in Harar a few days later without resistance. He positioned his troops outside the city and no pillaging took place. The monarch contented himself by slapping a fine of 75,000 thalers on the city and the countryside, and under the Abyssinian Law of War he confiscated the land and property of the conquered warriors killed in battle and took everything he wanted from the houses of the Europeans and everyone else. He demanded all weapons and munitions stored in the village, that had been previously owned by the Egyptian government, and he returned to Shoa leaving 3000 of his riflemen camped on a hill nearby. He entrusted the administration of the village to the uncle of Emir Abdullaï, Ali Abou Béker, whom the English took prisoner in Aden during the evacuation and was later made a slave in the house of his nephew.

Later on it came to pass that the Ali Abou Béker administration was not agreeable to Mékonène, Ménélik's chief representative, who descended on the village with his troops, lodging them in the houses and the mosques, then locking up Ali before sending him in chains to Ménélik.

The Abyssinians entered the village to reduce it to rubble, demolishing the houses, ravaging the plantations and terrorizing the population as only the negroes know how to do to each other. Meanwhile, Ménélik continued to send reinforcements from Shoa, followed by multitudes of slaves, while the number of Abyssinians actually in Harar probably numbered about 12,000, of which 4000 were riflemen armed with guns of all types, from Remingtons to flint-locks.

Collecting taxes in the surrounding region only happens through raids; villages are burned, livestock is stolen, and populations are taken away in slavery. Ever since the Egyptian government easily made off with 80,000 pounds from Harar, the Abyssinian treasury has been empty. Revenue from the Gallas, customs, trading posts and markets, and other proceeds, are stolen by anyone who can get at them. The people of the village are immigrating and the Gallas are not farming any more. In a few months the Abyssinians devoured the sorghum supply left by the Egyptians; it would have been enough for several years. Famine and plague are imminent.

The transactions of this market, in which location is very important, have ceased for the Gallas closest to the coast. The Abyssinians have prohibited the use of old Egyptian currency once used as change for thalers, for the exclusive privilege of a worthless copper currency. However, in Entotto I have seen some silver coins that Ménélik had his effigy cast into. He proposes to put these into circulation in Harar to settle the issue of currency.

Ménélik would love to keep Harar in his possession, but he knows that he is incapable of seriously running the country through collecting revenue and he knows that the English have looked unfavorably upon the Abyssinian occupation. They actually say that the Governor of Aden, who has always worked hard for the development of the British influence on the Somaliland coast, will do as much as he can to decide for his government whether to occupy Harar in case the Abyssinians expel him, which could happen through a famine or complications with the war in Tigré.

from absinthe to abyssinia

In Harar, from the Abyssinian point of view, they think they see the English troops appearing every morning on the mountain slopes. Mékonène has written to the English political representatives in Zeila and Berbera to not send any more of their soldiers to Harar. These representatives made sure each caravan was escorted by a few indigenous soldiers.

The English government, in response, has imposed a tax of 5% on all thalers entering Zeila, Boulhar and Berbera. This measure will contribute to the disappearance of this already very rare currency in Shoa and Harar, and it is doubtful that the import of rupees never seen in these regions will be favored. The English, for some reason, have also imposed an import tax of 1% on this coast.

Ménélik was strongly vexed by the prohibition of weapons on the coasts of Obock and Zeila. Since King John dreamed of having his seaport in Massaouah, Ménélik, even though he has been in exile far off in the interior, flatters himself by hoping to soon obtain a small outlet on the Gulf of Aden. Unfortunately, he wrote to the Sultan of Tadjoura after the establishment of the French protectorate and proposed selling his territory to him. Upon his entry into Harar, he declared himself ruler of all tribes from there to the coast and ordered his general, Mékonène, not to miss the opportunity of capturing Zeila. However, since the Europeans have spoken to Mékonène about artillery and warships, Ménélik's views on Zeila have changed; he recently wrote to the French government demanding the ceding of Ambado.

We know that the coast, from the bottom of the Gulf of Tadjoura to beyond Berbera, has been divided between France and England in the following manner: France gets the whole coastline of Goubbet Kérab to Djibouti, a cape located a dozen miles to the northwest of Zeila, and a strip of land quite a few kilometers into the interior where the boundary on the side of the English territory is formed by a line drawn from Djibouti to Ensa, the third trading station on the road from Zeila to Harar. Therefore, we have an outlet on the Harar/Abyssinia road. Ménélik aspires to own Ambado, a cove near Djibouti where the Governor of Obock, for a long time, has been sticking the tri-colored flag that the stubborn English agent from Zeila kept pulling out, until the negotiations were over. Ambado has no water, but Djibouti has some fine streams, and of the three stops on our road to Ensa, two have water.

In short, the formation of caravans can be a reality in Djibouti as soon as there is an establishment supplied with indigenous merchandise and armed troops. Until now, the place has been completely desolate. It goes without saying that a French port must be placed there if we want to compete with Zeila.

Zeila, Berbera and Bulhar remain with the English, as well as the Bay of Samawanak on the Gadiboursi coast, between Zeila and Bulhar, the point where the last representative from the French Consulate, M. Henry, stuck the tricolor, prompting the Gadiboursi tribe to ask for our protection, which they still enjoy. Over the last two years, such stories of annexations and protectorates have been raising spirits on this coast.

The successor of the French representative was M. Labosse, the French Consul in Suez, who was sent in the interim to Zeila, where he settled all disputes. There are now around 5000 French-protected Somalis in Zeila.

For Abyssinia, the road to Harar is quite advantageous. Whereas one arrives in Shoa by the Danakil road only after a journey of 50 to 60 days through a terrifying wasteland amidst a thousand dangers, Harar, in the foothills of the Ethiopian meridional mountains, is separated from the coast only by a distance easily traversed in fifteen days by caravan.

The road is very good, and the Issa tribe, accustomed to transport on it, is quite conciliatory. There is no danger from the neighboring tribes.

From Harar to Entotto, the actual residence of Ménélik, it is a twenty-day trek through the Itous Galla plateau at an altitude averaging 2500 meters, with provisions, means of transport and security guaranteed. In all, it takes a month to go from our coast to central Shoa, though the distance to Harar is only twelve days, and this latter place, in spite of invasions, is certainly destined to become the exclusive commercial outlet of Shoa and all Galla tribes. Ménélik himself was so struck by the advantageous position of Harar that upon his return, recalling the railway idea often suggested by Europeans, he began searching for someone to give the commission or concession to, from Harar to the sea. But then he changed his mind, remembering the presence of the English on the coast! It goes without saying that, in case this happens (and this will happen in the future, sooner or later), the government of Shoa will not contribute anything to the expenses of this project.

Ménélik completely lacks funds, always remaining in the most complete ignorance of (or indifference to) the exploitation of the region's resources that he forced into submission. He only thinks about accumulating guns in order to allow himself to send his troops to levy men from the Gallas. The few European traders who have gone to Shoa have brought to Ménélik, in total, 10,000 standard rifles and 15,000 percussion rifles in the space of five or six years. This was enough for the Amharans to make the neighboring Gallas submit.

Meanwhile in Harar, Dedjatch Mékonène proposes to descend on the Gallas and defeat them, all the way from their southern border to the coast of Zanzibar. He is even permitted to do this by Ménélik, who was made to believe that he could open a road in this direction for the importation of weapons. Since the Galla tribes are not armed, they can travel quite far from the coast.

Above all, what drives Ménélik to invade toward the south is the fake neighborliness and vexing lordship of King John. Ménélik has already left Ankober for Entotto. It is said that he wants to go down to Abba-Djifar, the most flourishing Galla region in Djimma, to establish his residence there. He has also talked about establishing himself in Harar. Ménélik dreams of the expansion of his domains to the south, beyond the Hawash, and is now considering leaving the Amharic areas that are part of the new Galla regions with his guns, his warriors and his wealth, to establish a meridional empire like the ancient kingdom of Ali Alaba, far away from the Emperor.

One wonders what is and what will be the attitude of Ménélik in the Italio-Abyssinian war. It is clear that his attitude will be determined by the will of his immediate neighbor King John, and not by the diplomatic means of governments at an unreachable distance from him — means he does not understand, yet nevertheless, is wary of. It is impossible for Ménélik to disobey King John, and the latter, well-informed of diplomatic plots when dealing with Ménélik, would do well to stay away from him. King John has already ordered him to choose his best soldiers, and Ménélik had to send them to the Emperor's camp in Asmara. In case of disaster, King John would retreat to Ménélik's territory. Shoa, the only Amharic country possessed by Ménélik, isn't worth one fifteenth of

Tigré. His other domains are all precariously submissive Galla regions and it would be very hard for him to avoid a general rebellion if he compromised himself in any way. One mustn't forget that patriotic sentiment does exist in Shoa, and with Ménélik as ambitious as he is, it's impossible that he doesn't see honor or advantage in listening to the advice of strangers.

He will therefore conduct himself in a way that will not compromise his already very embarrassing situation, and since these people do not understand, and since they only accept what they can see and touch, he will personally act according only to what the nearest neighbor will make him do, and nobody is more his neighbor than King John, who will make Ménélik avoid temptations. This is not to say that he does not listen compliantly to the diplomats; he will pocket what he can gain from them, and at an appointed time, King John, having been forewarned, will share with Ménélik. But, once again, the general patriotic sentiment and the opinion of Ménélik's people figure into the question. They do not want strangers, nor their meddling, nor their influence, nor their presence, under any pretext, no more in Shoa than in Tigré or in Galla.

Having promptly settled my business with Ménélik, I asked him for a promissory note in Harar, desirous as I was to travel the new road opened by the King through the Itous, a heretofore unexplored route that I attempted in vain to use at the time of the Egyptian occupation of Harar. At this time, M. Jules Borelli asked the King for permission to take a trip in this direction. Thus, I had the honor of traveling in the company of our kind and courageous compatriot whom I sent the entirely unpublished geodesic works on this region to, in Aden.

On this road there are seven stops on the other side of the Hawash, and twelve between Hawash and Harar on the Itou plateau, a magnificent region of pastures and splendid forests at an average altitude of 2500 meters, with a charming climate. The crops there are not widely spread, the population not being very dense — or perhaps these people strayed from the road in fear of the King's troops. Nonetheless, there are coffee plantations. The Itous supply the largest part of the few thousand tons of coffee annually sold in Harar. These regions are very healthy and fertile, and are the only ones in East Africa that have adapted to European colonization.

As for business in Shoa, there is currently nothing to import there, because of the arms prohibition on the coast. But anyone who can come up with 100,000 or so thalers can use them throughout the year to buy ivory and other merchandise, since there haven't been many exporters there for a few years and currency has become quite rare. There are opportunities, though. The new road is excellent and the political state of Shoa will not be disturbed by the war, as Ménélik is making sure, above all, to maintain order in his abode.

Most sincerely,

Rimbaud

Letter to Vice Consul Gaspary[28]

Aden, November 9, 1887

Monsieur,

I received your letter of the 8th and take note of your observations.

I am sending you the copy of the expenses of Labatut's caravan, but must keep the original because the caravan leader who signed it later stole part of the funds that the Azzaze gave him for the purchasing of camels. The Azzaze is stubborn about never paying the caravan expenses for the Europeans who can easily pay: the Danakils discovered the perfect opportunity to scandalize both the Azzaze and the foreigners there at the time, and every European there has seen the Bedouins take 75% on top of caravan expenses. Meanwhile, the Azzaze and Ménélik have been supporting the Bedouins in their conflicts with the foreigners since before the opening of the road to Harar.

Warned of all this, I had the idea of entrusting funds to my caravan leader. This did not stop him from taking me before the King right when I was departing, and asking for some 400 thalers in addition to the funds approved by him! On this occasion, he had for his lawyer *the dreadful bandit*

Mohammed Abou Béker, enemy of European travelers and traders in Shoa.

But the King, without considering the signature of the Bedouin (for paperwork is nothing at all in Shoa), and knowing that he lied, happened to insult Mohammed, who furiously struggled against me, then sentenced me to only pay a sum of 30 thalers and a Remington rifle: but I paid nothing at all. I later learned that the caravan leader had withdrawn 400 thalers from the Azzaze's own pocket, which was set aside for payments to the Bedouins, and that he had employed this money in the buying of slaves that he sent with the caravan of M. Savouré, M. Dimitri and M. Brémond, and they all died on the way. So Mohammed ran off to hide in Abba-Djifar, Djimma, where they say he died from dysentery. Thus, a month after my departure, the Azzaze had to reimburse those 400 thalers to the Bedouins — but if I would've been there he would've told him to pay me.

In all three instances, the most dangerous enemies of the Europeans are the Abou-Békers, because of their easy access to the Azzaze and the King, so as to slander us, disparage our ways and pervert our intentions. For the Danakil Bedouins, the Abou-Békers shamelessly set an example of theft, as they advise them in pillaging and murder. Impunity is guaranteed to the Abou-Békers by the Abyssinian and European authorities on the coasts, who crudely deceive each other. There are also some French in Shoa who get robbed on the road by Mohammed and are still subjected to his schemes, but nevertheless, they'll tell you: "Mohammed's a good boy!" even though the rest of the Europeans left in Shoa and Harar, aware of the politics and customs of the Abou-Békers (loathed by all the Danakil, Galla and Amharan people) still flee them like the plague.

The 34 Abyssinians in my escort had me good. In Sajalo, before departing, they made me sign an agreement to pay them 15 thalers each for the road, plus two months of back-pay, but in Ankober, annoyed by their insolent demands, I seized the paper and tore it up in front of them. Consequently, someone complained to the Azzaze, etc. Besides, we never take receipts for wages paid to servants in Shoa: they'd consider this act quite strange and believe themselves to be in danger of who knows what.

I wouldn't have paid the Azzaze the 300 thalers for Labatut if I didn't discover, in an old notebook found in Mme. Labutut's shack, an annotation in the writings of Labatut, showing a receipt from the Azzaze for almost 5 okiètes of ivory. Labatut was actually writing his *Mémoires*: I gathered 34 volumes, or 34 notebooks, in the home of his widow, and despite the cursings of the latter, I offered them to the flames. I was told this was a great misfortune. There were a few deeds inserted between these confessions, which briefly perused, did not appear worthy of serious examination.

Moreover, this Azzaze sycophant appeared in Farri with his burrows at the same time I was coming in with my camels, and immediately suggested to me, after exchanging greetings, that the foreigner I represented had a huge account with him, and he asked me for the entire caravan as security. I appeased him temporarily by offering him a telescope of mine and some bottles of candy-coated laxatives. I later sent him from afar what I thought he really deserved. He was bitterly disillusioned and always acted hostile toward me. Among other things, he stopped the other sycophant, a high priest, from paying me for a load of raisins that I brought him for making homemade wine for Mass.

As for the various debts I paid for Labatut, it happened in the following manner:

A Dedjatch came to my house and sat down to drink my meed, boasting of the noble qualities of his *friend* (the late Labutut!), while expressing the hope of discovering the same virtues in me. Upon seeing a mule grazing on the lawn, he declared, "There's that mule I gave to Labatut!" (he neglected to mention that the cloak he was wearing was also given to him by Labatut!). "Besides," he added, "he owes me 70 thalers (or 50, or 60, etc.!)" He insisted on this demand so much that I dismissed the noble bandit by telling him, "Go to the King!" (which is pretty much to say "Go to the Devil!"). But the King made me pay part of the claim, hypocritically adding that he would pay the rest!

But I have paid on some legitimate claims as well. For example, I paid the wages of Labatut's dead servants to their wives. There were also some reimbursements of 30, 15 and 12 thalers, to some peasants that Labatut took money from, promising them guns, fabric, etc., in return. Since these poor people are always of good faith, I felt for them and I paid. I was also ordered to pay a sum of 20 thalers to M. Dubois. I saw that this was just and I paid, adding a pair of my shoes for interest. The poor devil had been complaining about going barefoot.

The news of my virtuous behavior started spreading far and wide. There arose, here and there, a series of Labatut's creditors, in groups, in hordes, with their embarrassing routines, and this modified my benevolent disposition. I became determined to hurry up and get out of Shoa. I remember the morning of my departure: while trotting toward the NNE I saw an emissary of a wife of a friend of Labatut leap from a bush, requesting from me, in the name of the Virgin Mary, a sum of 19 thalers. Then, further on, appearing on top of a cliff, a strange individual in a sheepskin cloak asked me if I paid 12 thalers to his brother that were borrowed from Labatut, etc. I yelled at these people that it was too late!

When I was going to Ankober, Labatut's widow began proceedings against me with the Azzaze in a scathing trial hinging on her claim of inheritance. M. Hénon, a French explorer, made himself her lawyer in this noble task, and he summoned me and dictated to the widow the statement of his pretensions with the aid of two old-lady Arab attorneys. After odious debates wherein I sometimes had the upper hand, and sometimes the lower, the Azzaze ordered me to seize the houses of the deceased. But the widow had already hidden a few thalers of merchandise, personal effects and curios left by him. During the seizure of these things, which didn't happen without resistance, I found some old pairs of underwear that the old widow took with impassioned tears along with some bullet molds and a dozen pregnant slaves I declined.

M. Hénon began proceedings for an appeal on behalf of the widow, and the Azzaze, dumbfounded, left it to the judgement of the foreigners in Ankober. My business already appearing disastrous, M. Brémond then decided that I would only have to give up the land, gardens and livestock of the deceased to this shrew, and that upon my departure, the Europeans would collect a sum of 100 thalers to give to the wife. M. Hénon, representing the plaintiff, put himself in charge of the operation and stayed in Ankober.

The eve of my departure from Entotto, going up to the monarch's with M. Ilg to get the bill from the Dedjatch of Harar, I saw behind me in the mountains the helmet of M. Hénon, who, aware of my departure, rapidly traversed the

120 kilometers from Ankober to Entotto. And behind him I saw the cloak of the frenetic widow winding along the precipice. At the King's, I waited a few hours in the antechamber as *they* desperately appealed to him. But when I was introduced, M. Ilg swiftly told me that *they* did not succeed. The monarch declared that he had been the friend of Labatut and that he had intended to pursue his friendship with his descendants, and to prove it, he immediately withdrew the fruits of the land from the widow, which he had given to Labatut!

M. Hénon's goal was to make me pay the 100 thalers that he *himself* had to collect from the Europeans for the widow. I learned that after my departure the deal was never finalized!

M. Ilg, because of his knowledge of languages and his honesty, is employed by the King in the basic handling of European affairs with the royal court. He made me understand that Ménélik pretended that Labatut was deeply in debt to him. Actually, the day when my capital was calculated, Ménélik said that Labatut owed him quite a lot, so I responded by demanding evidence. It was a Saturday and the King replied that we should consult the accounts. On Monday, after having unrolled the archival scrolls, the King declared that he had discovered a sum of about 3500 thalers, which he expressed should be subtracted from my account. In addition to this, he declared that realistically, all Labatut's goods should be returned to him. All this came from a tone that could not be refuted. I noted the European creditors and finally my credit, and due to the objections of M. Ilg, the King hypocritically consented to drop $3/8$ths of his demand.

I am convinced that the Abyssinian Emperor stole from me and that his merchandise is circulating on roads that I am still condemned to wander. I hope I can get it back one day for the value of what he owes me, and likewise, I must get a hold of Ras Govana for a sum of 600 thalers in case he persists in his demands, since I heard that the King spoke to him about keeping quiet; this is what he always says after he has already paid himself.

Such is the situation, Monsieur Consul, of my payments on the debts of Labatut's caravan to the natives. Excuse me for doing it in this manner, to distract myself from the nature of the memories this affair created for me, which are, all in all, very disagreeable.

With my utmost respect,

Rimbaud

Aden, February 1, 1888

Dear Monsieur Ilg,

I was glad to receive your letter of January 16. I hope you are experiencing peace and good health.

I regret that your methods have been useless. I knew this would happen, we expected it. The hopes entertained by the gun sellers in their memorandums were simply bait meant to catch our funds if we had been as stupid as them, which is not permitted here.

I made the deputies in my department take action with the present Minister of the Navy and Colonies who is also from the city of my birth. All this was a complete failure: I have lost nothing to this, however, because I didn't hope for anything and I didn't run up any bills.

Your predictions on the saga of Massaouah are those of everyone here. They will conquer all volcanic mammaries within 30 kilometers of Massaouah, connect them with shoddy railways, and when they arrive in these extremities, they'll blast their howitzers at the buzzards and launch a zeppelin streamered with heroic slogans — and that'll be it. This will then be the moment to throw out the last few hundred of the several thousand camels and burrows recently bought here, as well as the boards from the huts, etc., and all that crappy material which their military proudly worked for.

But after this moment of legitimate delirium, what will happen? Many will want to maintain the beautiful Massaouah plain. The conquest will generate expenses and it will be dangerous to preserve it. It is true that their guards keep watch, armed with machine-guns.

The idiotic Reuter Agency announced to us this morning that the Turkish government has requested the English to evacuate Zeila immediately! What's behind this? — I think the Turkish Mission has probably demanded the Harar region from the Emperor. — Anyway, for Zeila, the English have naturally responded that they will consult the Egyptian Viceroy first, since he lives in the Turkish-controlled city of Zeila.

For a long time you've known that Mékonène left Harar and that nobody knows when he's coming back. There are only about 800 men left under a native chief there, so they say. The road is not bad.

Bienenfeld is sending a political agent to Harar. These types are quite annoying with the way they indecently expose themselves to Ethiopia. This agent has been in Zeila for a month without daring to hit the road.

Stephen the Armenian (the trader) has passed through here again. He has no complaint at all against King Ménélik and is ready to return again. He left to buy some merchandise in Egypt.

Stephen second-class has some red and green goatskins here. He's not very strong because he still has a fever.

After you left, M. Bion sold Brémond's ivory for 215 or 216 rupees. — Ivory is going up, musk is at 3 thalers.

No matter what's being said, I believe that nothing can

stop Soleillet's guns from leaving now. Moreover, if the people in charge of the deal can be stopped, they can take the opportunity to be compensated for it.

Other than that, there's nothing new, except that an English officer and thirty or so soldiers were killed the day before yesterday near Berbera.

The news from Shoa, despite what's said, is good. Ménélik did some grimacing, but things are still the same for everyone.

— I am leaving for the coast in about a week. I might stay in the interior for two or three months. I would like to see if an exploration for gum could be undertaken in the lowlands of Harar, in Gadiboursi, etc.... There are many gum trees there and I have guides throughout the area.

— The members of Soleillet's caravan are panicking, they aren't receiving any news and will be on the coast for a long time if they don't get cracking.

— I hear that the borders of the Issa coasts between France and England will be established. Djibouti should remain with the English. Ambado is a very French place and the Governor of Obock would be happy if they opened it for him.

— There is a risk that the blockades will continue even during the ceasing of hostilities in the vicinity of Massaouah, and after the troops return. All these raids, explorations, requisitions, prohibitions and persecutions make the natives irritated and resentful, on the coasts as well as in the interior. All this is badly organized and badly calculated if the Europeans, who are already quite despised on the Red Sea, are to be redeemed in the eyes of the negroes. — The moral: to remain allies with the negroes or not to mess with them at all, if they cannot be completely crushed in the first place.

— At the moment, it is certainly wise to observe events in Abyssinia and not take any direct action. — For me, if I return to African soil it will be no farther than Harar, because ultimately, commerce is free there and we can flee when we want.

— We will see. It is said that some merchandise is currently going for a good price in Shoa and that export merchandise is available at a very good price.

— Dimitri sends his greetings to you: he recently retrieved almost everything that was lost.

— With regard to the ivory of Dedjatch W. Gabril, I am told that it's been sold here by my Danakil guide who spent all the money buying merchandise for the Dedjatch and himself. But I also hear that M. Hénon allegedly has some thalers for the Dedjatch. I don't know if this is true or false — but the Danakil and the Abyssinian who came down with the ivory are presently at each others' throats.

Take care, Monsieur, so I may have the pleasure of seeing you again.

All my best,

Rimbaud

Address: c/o Camp Aden.

Letter to Ilg

Aden, March 29, 1888

Dear Monsieur Ilg,

On returning from Harar after fifteen days I found your friendly letter. Thank you.

I made the trip to Harar in six days, five days on the way back, then spent eight days up there and ten days on sailing ships and steamers (this was the longest and most boring part of it), making for a month-long journey.

Good news up there. There is peace on earth beneath the tranquil skies. The doctors doctor (while their wives get raped, which is what happened to the good Signor Traversi who reportedly disowned his lawful-wedded wife and kept the kid). Sig. Alfieri has gone back to Shoa and Sig. Antonelli to Lit-Marefia. M. Borelli went to Djimma, M. Brémond is on his way to Harar, Sig. Viscardi is going to Aoussa, M. Bidault and his luggage are en route to Harar and Herr Zimmermann has now gone back to Harar with a three-tiered helmet-hat. They have begun to clean up in Harar, but it looks like they will soon drop dead from hunger.

As you know, M. Lagarde built some shacks in Djibouti and is watching the whole coast in expectation of M. Savouré, even though the road is not yet open.

I am going back to Harar again very soon to represent the traders of Aden. I will be the only Frenchman in Harar.

Consequently, I am naturally your contact and I claim the privilege of serving you in any way that may be useful in your operations there.

In Zeila my contact will be a Greek, M. Sotiro, an honest lad who knows the country well.

Watch out in the bar in Mousaïa.

Monsieur Tian will correspond with me in Aden and Monsieur Bardey as well.

— Be very cautious (please heed my advice and excuse me for this), the coast is in a total state of siege.

Rimbaud
c/o the French Consulate
Zeila, Red Sea

or:
c/o Monsieur Tian
Aden.

Letter to Ugo Ferrandi[30]

Steamer Point, Aden
April 2, 1888

Dear Sir,

I have prepared everything in order to leave on the "Tuna," which will arrive Saturday. You can do the same and avoid needless packing. I gladly accept traveling together and am counting on our quick and easy arrival.

My best to you,

Rimbaud

P.S. It is unnecessary to speak of my departure to anyone.

— Rd.

from absinthe to abyssinia

Letter to His Mother and Sister

Aden, April 4, 1888

Dear friends,

I received your letter of March 19. I am returning from a trip to Harar. I did 600 kilometers in eleven days on horseback.

I am leaving again in three or four days for Zeila and Harar, where I will definitely establish myself. I am representing the traders of Aden.

It's been a long time since the reply came from the Minister of the Navy and Colonies, and it was negative as I predicted. There is nothing that can be done on this side, but in any case, I have found something else.

I will therefore live in Africa again and will not be seen for a long time. Let's hope this business gets settled with as little trouble as possible.

So, from now on, write to me in care of my contact in Aden and avoid any compromising information in your letters. My best to you — Monsieur Rimbaud

c/o Monsieur César Tian
— Aden —
English domains
Arabia.

You can also, and preferably even, write to me directly in Zeila, this place being part of the Postal Union (find out about postage).

Monsieur Arthur Rimbaud in Zeila
Red Sea
via Aden
English domains.

Letter to Ugo Ferrandi

Aden, April 10, 1888

Dear Monsieur Hugo,

I heard that the "Toona" will not leave until Thursday afternoon.

In any case, I will count on you being ready.

Since I am embarking from Mallah, be so good as to take *M. Rondani's two cases*, which are on the veranda at Suel's, along with your baggage, and get them on board. I will pay the expenses on his behalf.

Otherwise, I am afraid those cases will no longer be there in a few more years.

My best to you,

Rimbaud

Letter to Ilg

Aden, April 12, 1888

Dear Monsieur,

Monsieur Tian will give you this letter as you pass through Aden, and will affirm that I am his contact in Harar and neighboring countries. Tomorrow I am going to Zeila. I should be in Harar toward the end of this month, supplied with capital and merchandise.

I am entirely at your service for all your messages, shipments, storage, errands and negotiations that you might like to avail yourself of in central Harar and on the roads going there. The offer is completely separate from business and I am letting Monsieur Tian know this as well. He will make himself completely available to you in Aden. — My contact in Zeila is a Greek named Sotiro who you can stay with when you go there. I asked him to do everything he can for you in Zeila and to help you get on the road.

Allow me to caution you not to trust the house of Moussaya for anything. They are a band of spies who specialize in studying the ways of everyone who goes there, so as to get them in all kinds of trouble.

I am hoping that my new business in Harar will expand as much as time and place allow, and that later on, with me in Harar and you in Shoa, with your exceptional experience with people and languages and things, we can organize something profitable for both of us.

So if you write to someone in Harar, do me the pleasure and write to me as well. I await your safe arrival. Devotedly yours,

Rimbaud
at Mr. Sotiro's*
Zeila
Red Sea, Gulf of Aden.

* He will forward my mail to me with promptness and security.

Letter to Ugo Ferrandi

Harar, April 30, 1889

Dear Monsieur Ferrandi,

I have received your ticket from Gueldessah and have communicated your message to Naufragio, who sends his greetings to you.

You probably know how the Abyssinians have been using your house after you left. This is something that should not surprise you.

A soldier will probably meet you in Biokaboba. Nothing new here: the orgies of Easter week are over: it is still St. Joyés week.

The Abyssinians are getting a caravan ready to go to Shoa tomorrow or the day after, which will leave with Khawaga Elias and the imposing Mossieu Moskoff. — No news from Shoa for a month. The Greeks who came from Zeila say King John is dead. It's probably in the Corazzini telegrams, but the natives here don't know anything about it.

Say hello to your companion, tell him he will now be looked after (4th day). I wrote to Tian's agent in Zeila to ask if he could lodge with him.

Enclosed is a ticket for him.

All my best,

Rimbaud

from absinthe to abyssinia

Letter to Ilg

Harar, September 7, 1889
Via Ibrahim

My Dear Monsieur Ilg,

I am confirming my last letter to you "via Akader," which was taken to Shoa and should have reached you by now, containing an invoice for 81 packages of merchandise valued at 1,987,375 thalers, loaded on 24 camels entrusted to your two servants, who have also received from me a more than sufficient payment for all traveling and lodging expenses. I think this merchandise will reach you in Farri a few days after this message arrives.

M. Savouré wrote me from Koricati-Hérer on the 27th of August and I guess he has now arrived in Djibouti. He informed me that you have complete power to liquidate his business in Shoa, but depending on the news you give him he'll see if he should ask me to send you the balance of the payment, or if I should present him with a bill. From Aden he will then give me his instructions on this subject.

My last shipment sent "via Akader" contained four letters for M. Savouré in your envelope. You can send them back to me, I will forward them.

Mohammed has left M. Savouré in Hérer and has come here to deliver his merchandise being held in customs. He is going to go down to the coast, perhaps with M. Bortoli, M. Brémond's associate — who is leaving for Djibouti with the caravan of merchandise bought here by both associates, while M. Brémond goes up to Shoa.

Since the 1000 thalers I sent to you via Engadda, I have absolutely not been able to dig up any money for your account, despite various steps taken and numerous protests, and in reading what follows you will soon understand why.

King Ménélik (who gave him this damned idea!) wrote here about a month ago to collect an outrageous tax of *100,000 thalers.* — He could have ordered the extortion of this sum through all means possible, and he even added that he could borrow from the Europeans while promising to repay them from the funds which Dedjatch Mékonène may or may not bring. — Since then, we have been witness to a spectacle here which the country has never seen, not during the time of the emirs, nor during the time of the Turcs — a horrible, odious tyranny which will most likely dishonor all of Amhara for a long time on all coasts and in all regions here, a dishonor that will surely stain the name of the King.

For a month, the people of the village have been sequestered, beaten, imprisoned and dispossessed of their property, in order to extort as much of the demanded sum as possible. Each inhabitant has already paid three or four times during this period. All the Europeans associated with the Muslims are subject to this tax. They have demanded 200 thalers from me of which I have paid half, and I am afraid they will extort the remaining 100 from me even though they have also forced me to lend them 4000 thalers in the most arbitrary, thieving manner — this incident is the subject of the enclosed request and I would be forever indebted to you if you would

from absinthe to abyssinia

present it to the King on my behalf. — I always ask you for help and I strongly regret not being able to give you the money, but anyway, believe me, I am here and yours devotedly. If you need anything, I am completely at your service.

Around the end of August, a few days after having paid the tax of 100 thalers, I received 10,000 thalers in four cashboxes from M. Tian in Zeila. Upon the arrival of the camels in customs, I prepared myself to receive delivery, but a representative of Mékonène's wife and Tessamma ordered the customs officer to seize everything. I tried to protest, but they refused to either see me or speak to me in the King's palace, nor would they explain to me the reason why they seized the sum, whether as a loan or something else. It was only with the energetic intervention of Monseigneur Taurin that I was able to receive delivery of the four cashboxes the following day. Since I was already prepared to send a letter to the Consul in Aden requesting him to send a telegram to the embassy in Rome, and in that I was also ready to handle the affair diplomatically and judicially, Monseigneur explained to them that such an act of piracy would probably expose Mékonène to some reprisals on his property as well as his person, either on the coast or in Europe.

Nevertheless, *they forced me to loan* a sum of 4000 thalers, of which I obtained a receipt through great difficulty. This obligates the Dedjatch to reimburse me upon his return!

At the same time, funds for various other Europeans arrived in lesser quantities and the same thing happened to them — *borrowing* 500, or 600 or 300 thalers from each of them without providing any receipts, guarantees or terms for reimbursement!

The English soldiers who accompanied the funds here have

left to carry this news to Zeila along with stories of extortion practiced on the natives. The consequences of this will be tremendous and will completely discourage my associates in Aden, I'm afraid, even though I clearly explained the situation to them.

Plus, this loan really bothered me because those 4000 thalers could have been changed for the latest Egyptian currency and I could have reimbursed M. Savouré for the coffee I obtained for around this amount.

I tried to keep the said sum in my cashbox by offering some IOUs worth 3000 thalers from Savouré, and the other 1000 from you, but those surly dogs demanded payment in cash from me — so I paid.

Under these circumstances you can see that it is *momentarily* impossible for me to obtain anything for your two accounts. Instead of paying, they're stealing! — All possible proceeds go exclusively into paying taxes. The coffee in customs is only sold for cash, and thalers at that! The situation is abominable! And despite the unreasonable demands for 100,000 thalers, the King is sending new creditors here to collect payments daily! Mohammed was recently here again with a bill from the King for a few thousand thalers! *Instead of paying him*, two packets of money were *BORROWED* from him in customs; these were being held for my debt ever since they arrived in Djibouti two months ago!

With all these extortions, I doubt that we can gather more than 30,000 thalers which need to be sent in a few days by boat via Tchertcher. The situation is actually very sad in this region: animal epidemics have destroyed everything, the coffee harvest is bad, importing is quite weak this year — and finally, it should be noted that it has scarcely been four months since the annual tax was paid and it'll start up again in three months! — And the debts for Harar's treasury are continually increasing along with the demands of the King! — We fear mass plundering!

It would be good if someone made the King understand that the conduct of his people here is detrimental for him as well. The place is quite close to the coast, the population is constantly involved with the administrators of various governments in the Gulf of Aden and surrounding areas, and there are plenty estranged subjects here, as well as quite a few protected natives, not to mention French, English, Italian and Ottoman subjects. Everywhere on the coast now, the Bedouins, the poor, the merchants, the consuls, the residents, and the officers are talking about what's happening in Harar, where the coffers of the European traders in Aden are being robbed and the inhabitants are being pulled from their homes at midnight to sweat a few thalers under threat of getting whipped to death. Still, there is no fear of revolt here, with the people completely disarmed and reduced to powerlessness for their own good. Yet the moral effect in the interior and on the outside will be more pernicious for the Amharans than a native uprising.

I will do all I can so our political representatives and traders know how we are vilified here, but I doubt that they will renounce their complacent politics!

What more can I say in the midst of these lugubrious preoccupations? Do me the actual honor, I repeat, of seeing that the enclosed request is delivered to the King and translated by Gabriel or someone else in a faithful manner — and finish the job by reminding the King to give me a reply which will hopefully distinguish me from the bandits here.

You can see that my epistle has a postscript concerning

you. In expectation, I am still counting on getting something for you in merchandise or even in Egyptian piastres that I will only accept with the certainty of an even exchange. As for M. Savouré's account, I will close it by force, as I have said before. You have no idea of the grimaces, the screams, of the clowning I must do in order to finagle a few hundred thalers, or rather, what appear to be thalers — because I hardly ever see *true thalers*! When you see Brémond, maybe he will play the matador by speaking of his exploits here, but know that he will bitterly remember the coffers and customs of Harar, and that he will never return here again. Besides, out of the 9000 thalers the Dedjatch owes him, not even 3000 thalers have been paid to him in four months.

For the moment though, we must let the flurry of the royal tax pass. Anyway, the question has already been decided. There are only about 30,000 thalers to be found here, so we have to abandon the operation. — What can be found will be sent and the country will be left in peace. So let's send it... to the Devil!

All this is highly discouraging to me and if it continues it will be impossible for me to endure it. I wonder how I can exist here knowing that I am being robbed daily and being forced to loan money to a government that owes me money, etc., etc.... I am asking the King for a letter of protection permitting me to conduct business freely while paying the country's taxes. But I want to stay ready to liquidate, and for the moment, I am hoping to put away a small amount of merchandise for import, which I still have, to collect what I am owed. Do everything possible to send me, toward the end of the year, or by February 1890 at the latest, the money for the merchandise I sent you. If I send you anything, it will only be articles of little value.

from absinthe to abyssinia

> *Once again, for all the merchandise you send, get a pass from the King for transport, otherwise you will have some terrible stories to tell about being in customs here:*

Taxes will be evaluated without their immediate payment, but sooner or later they will be put on your account. Therefore, address your merchandise to me "allegedly in transit," and with the royal pass it will enter and exit without any trouble. Otherwise, ivory pays 8 thalers per load upon entry, 6 thalers on departure (on the spot). Musk pays 10% upon entry and 2% on departure. Gold never passes through customs, but if it were discovered it wouldn't miss being taxed. All this is completely absurd because Harar is connected with Shoa — it is not an independent administration. We have explained a hundred times that all entry taxes should be completely abolished and should be replaced by a general exit tax of 5% for a hundred different reasons; this would generate much more revenue.

— Musk is always falling. It is presently at $1^1/2$ thalers here, but I wouldn't want it at that price, since the "prospects" in Europe are deplorable.

— Ivory is stable at 95 to 105 thalers in Aden.

— Pure gold rings are at *20 thalers here*. I buy.

— I asked for some of your nitric acid about 50 days ago in Aden, and your letters have been sent.

I put them in the Azzaze's package.

I look forward to hearing from you.

Rimbaud

Letter to Ilg

Harar, September 18, 1889

Dear Monsieur Ilg,

This letter comes by way of M. Brémond.

The messenger Ibrahim, who will come at the same time as M. Brémond, has three letters from me for you, one of them containing an urgent request for the King for a sum of 4000 thalers that have been *BORROWED BY FORCE* from me in the palace, to give to the King under the pretext of paying me back with the funds that Antonelli, or rather Dedj. Mékonène, might bring, for I doubt that Antonelli will return. — Enclosed is another epistle to the King confirming the first. Make sure it reaches him.

Nothing of interest is happening. About 40,000 thalers have been sent to the King from here, collected through much injustice and misery of which we have had our share! We are in the hands of bandits here. — How will it end?

Dedj. Mékonène is strolling around in Italy. They will send you to Emir Abdulai in Ankober. — Everyone here is telling us that Mékonène will be replaced. We would really be interested if you could tell us who the choice might be. — We have been left here in complete ignorance, it is quite disconcerting.

from absinthe to abyssinia

The Italians are fortifying themselves in Asmara and in Kéren, I think they are getting reinforcements now.

I have still not received a response on your acid.

I guess it's in Zeila.

My best to you,

Rimbaud

P.S. With all this, don't be surprised not to find any mention of your payment. Only stealing goes on here, never paying.

Rb.

Harar, October 7, 1889

My dear Monsieur Ilg,

I have received your two letters from Aibamba on September 10 and Ankober on September 16, as I have received all your previous letters.

[. . . .]

I am sending the enclosed copy of the bill for the saucepans back to you. I am guessing that the caravan has returned to you by now and I hope your men haven't died on the way.

[. . . .]

For the merchandise I sent to you through Jean, your observations are right on. Anyway, from the total sale of all those knick-knacks, I think there will be some profit for you. The large pearls are good for Lekka, etc., etc.... — I could give you some lessons on Ethiopian commercial geography.

[. . . .]

Finally, through grunts and grimaces, you will be paid, I hope, though there are some moments when I despair too. — The specific cause of all these delays, as you well know, is due to the exasperating actions of the King himself.

Enclosed is a collection of short articles concerning the Shoan mission. I will send you everything I receive of this kind. They have probably left Italy by now and are on their way to Jerusalem, Bethlehem and Sodom and Gomorrah — I don't think they'd miss the chance to visit these Holy places. They reportedly won't pass through Aden again, which they detest from being there before. Anyway, in a few days, some soldiers will be sent to the coast to receive them.

[. . . .]

It would please me, and you would do me a great favor, if you could give me as much information as you can about how this region is regarded. Everyone's certain that Dedjatch Mékonène will not stay in Italy and will soon plan his return. Then what will happen here? I hear the special forces from Tigré will return to Shoa and that the Dedjatch's people will return with him, so who will stay here? Will the Dedjatch be replaced, and by whom? Fifteen days ago, Emir Abdullah was sent to Shoa — what the devil do they want to do with him up there? — With a thousand soldiers here we can rest easy, but the road from Shoa must be open or business here will go bad and the revenues of the village will diminish incredibly as we witnessed last year....

The soldiers receiving the Dedjatch in Zeila have not left yet. Mail arrived yesterday from Aden with a telegram from Italy announcing the departure of the embassy, which was planned for the end of September. Nonetheless, I think they are leaving today.

In the last letter there were a few short articles on the Shoan mission. — Do as you please with them.

You can see that the extortions practiced on the city of Harar are widely known, even in Europe. If I wasn't established here, I would send some interesting details on the economic situation of these regions to the *Times*, concerning the Shoan mission and the way Dedj. Mékonène pays his debts, and the way King Ménélik sends his debtors to fall flat on their faces!

But let's keep quiet about these disgraces!

[. . . .]

— Yesterday they promised me they would weigh 100 loads of coffee this morning, half for your account, half for Savouré's. But this morning they told me that they took the coffee back in order to stick it on some skinflint in payment for nails furnished for the carpentry of their damn basilica.

Besides this, I can't even raise a thaler, since all the revenue (after the final payment to the King) isn't enough to finish paying our end-of-the-year payment.

Therefore, there's nothing to do but be patient!....

Rimbaud

Letter to Ilg

Harar, December 11, 1889
Via Serquis.
Letter No. 12.

My dear Monsieur Ilg,

Again, I am taking advantage of the opportunity to use Serquis to send you a package of some more or less antiquated newspapers; for an inhabitant of Shoa this can always be of interest.

I have received (I forgot to tell you in No. 11) your letter through Elias. — As for the reproach you gave me for starving men and beasts in transit, that's a laugh! On the contrary, I am known all over for my generosity in such cases — but that's typical of the recognition you get from the natives!

Hello to M. Zimmermann. Greetings to M. Brémond. Write more. My best to you,

Rimbaud

Letter to His Mother and Sister

Harar, January 3, 1890

My dear mother and sister,

I received your letter of November 19, 1889. You tell me you have received nothing from me since a letter of May 18th! That's too much; I write you almost every month, I even wrote to you in December wishing you prosperity and health for 1890, which I now have the pleasure of repeating to you.

As for your letters every couple weeks, be assured that I would never let one go by without responding to it, but nothing has reached me. I am very upset about this and will demand an explanation in Aden where I am amazed they were lost.

All my best, your son and brother,

Rimbaud
Chez Monsieur Tian
Aden, Arabia
English Colonies.

from absinthe to abyssinia

Letter to King Ménélik[31]

Letter from Monsieur Rimbaud,
import/export trader in Harar,
to His Majesty King Ménélik
entrusted to the goodwill
of Monsieur Ilg

Your Majesty,

How are you? Please accept my sincere salutations and best wishes.

The chiefs, or rather, the chief bandits of Harar, refuse to return the 4000 thalers they took from my coffers in your name under the pretext of a loan. It has been seven months since then.

I have already written to you three times on this subject.

This money is the property of French merchants on the coast. They sent it to me to conduct business with on their behalf in this region, and now they have seized everything I have on the coast and they want to take this agency away from me.

I estimate a 2000-thaler loss that this affair has cost me *personally*. — What do you want to give me for this loss?

Furthermore, each month I pay 1% interest on this money, and have already paid 280 thalers from my own pocket for the sum that you are keeping from me as interest accrues each month.

In the name of justice, I beg you to return the 4000 thalers to me as soon as possible, in actual thalers like I lent, and all the interest of 1% per month as well, from the day of the loan to the day of reimbursement.

I am making a full report of this affair to our leaders in Obock and to our Consul in Aden, so they will know how we are treated in Harar.

Please respond to me as soon as possible.

Harar, April 7, 1890.

Rimbaud
French trader in Harar

from absinthe to abyssinia

[April 1890]

. . . .

I have no need for your disgusting coffee, purchased at the price of a lot of trouble for the Abyssinians; I only took it so you could finish paying me off, since you were in such a rush. Moreover, and I will say it again, if I wouldn't have proceeded in such a way, you *never would've gotten anything for it — Nothing, absolutely nothing, Nothing Nothing Nothing*, and everyone knows it, including you! But I see that the air of Djibouti has made you lose your mind!

Therefore, after having transported *that rubbish at my own risk,* without any benefit at all, I would have been a cretin and an idiot to import thalers here for the white account at 2% of the transport cost, with a 2 or 3% loss in the exchange rate, to reimburse you for coffee I never asked for, which will bring me nothing in return, etc., etc. Are you capable of understanding this?

The people leaving Shoa are truly of Abyssinian mentality!

Therefore, dear sir, examine my accounts and consider things in their true light, and you will see that I am in the right — and that you are lucky to have ended up as you have!

Therefore, please send a receipt as soon as possible for *8333 thalers for the balance on all accounts* — and no more fooling around — because I could easily charge you for a few thousand thalers in losses I suffered due to your business practices I should have never been involved in.

In expectation of your receipt, please accept my sincere salutations.

Rimbaud

Excerpts from a Letter to Ilg

Harar, September 20, 1890

My dear Ilg,

I received your letter of August 23rd through M. Davico.

[. . . .]

I strongly doubt that he [Zimmermann] will reimburse the difference for the coffee and customs, but he will come up with 500 thalers, as he is known to do, from repeatedly demanding payments and by constantly looking for a discount. It seems that he has become more and more horribly stingy! Moreover, he is mired in increasingly terrible troubles that would take too long for me to describe to you.

[. . . .]

Like you, I would be very glad to see that stock liquidated as soon as possible. I would be even more pleased than you, and the latter part of this letter will tell you why. Therefore, give what you wish to the King, as you wish, *may the payment be immediate* — and to the Devil with what you want, and on the same terms! Let's get it over with, provided that (I repeat) it's done *in cash*, without hesitating over the loss of a few hundred thalers on the invoice value. This is what I have always told you. I have confidence in what you will do. *I am absolutely counting on receiving the product of this stock before December, for I will surely have to leave at the end of the year* and will have to completely liquidate my business with Tian.

— And now, pay serious attention to what follows, it is in your personal interest:

For the last two months, there has been an enormous revolution in the exchange rate of the rupee and the thaler. Silver has gone up incredibly, due to a certain "Silver Bill" passed in the United States to reestablish the monetary equilibrium. Hence, the U.S. has been minting millions of dollars of silver each month. It's not a question of a momentary crisis — silver won't drop any lower in the next few years. The rupee (which used to go up 5 centimes at a time) is now worth 2.3 francs and will soon go up to 2.5. The thaler is now at 5 francs, and will go up even more. The guinea is currently at 11 rupees, the Napoleon is at 9, etc.... This year will be disastrous.

[. . . .]

— I believe I have done well to warn you! Enclosed are six letters for you and one for M. Appenzeller.

Rushed salutations,

Rimbaud

As for the coffee, Moussaya never spoke of it to me.

from absinthe to abyssinia

Harar, November 20, 1890

My dear Ilg,

One final last-minute word.

Find me a very good MULE (not a small mule, but *a mule*), young, big, well-behaved, strong, a good climber, etc., etc., the best that can be found: price is no object, you can go up to 60 thalers for a very good one, which you can find among the chiefs you know. Send it to me with the men I am waiting for, to settle our account, in six weeks or two months.

Take a good shot at unloading all my merchandise and send me what you make. Excuse me for having inconvenienced you: I hope you will gain something from my junk. If I didn't send everything at the time of the balance of your account, it was because I didn't want the amount to appear too obvious in the semi-monthly inventories that Tian demands of me. Besides, with the money you're receiving from my hardware, sewing-supply and curio stores, etc., you can buy things you can always profit from, the difference between our price and that in Aden being scarcely 6 to 10%.

We estimate ivory ($37^1/2$ pounds) to be between 100 to 108 thalers, *firm*. Musk 1 thaler per quarter ounce, *not much in demand.* Gold $17^1/2$ to 18 thalers (But *don't rely on gold,* which can fall again if the rupee rises). The Harari coffee costs from $5^1/2$ to 6 now, but it will probably fall. Abyssinian coffee would therefore cost 9 thalers now.

They say the Ras is supposed to come to Shoa with Antonelli, who is expected here in a few days. These continual absences of the Governor are deplorable. We are at the mercy of minor chiefs who are as voracious as crocodiles, and Muslims looking for any excuse to do us harm.

— The politicians of Aden foresee some complications in Abyssinia. The Italians, not being able to get Kassala from the English, are occupying the border of Mareb, etc., etc.

Sincerely yours,

Rimbaud

from absinthe to abyssinia

Notes of the Damned[33]

Tuesday, April 7, 1891.

Left Harar at 6 in the morning. Arrived in Degadallal at 9:30 a.m. Swamp to Upper Egon, 12 o'clock. Egon to Fort Ballawa, 3 o'clock. Descent from Egon to Ballawa very hard on us. The carriers stumbled over every pebble, almost dumping me every step of the way. The stretcher was half broken and the men were completely exhausted. Tried to ride a mule, my bad leg slung from its neck. Had to get off after a few minutes and get back on the stretcher, which was already a kilometer behind. Arrived in Ballawa. It rained. Furious wind all night.

Wednesday the 8th.

Left Ballawa at 6:30. Got to Gueldessah at 10:30. The carriers did better and all that was left to suffer was the descent from Ballawa. Storm at 4 o'clock in Gueldessah.

Night, heavy with dew and cold.

Thursday the 9th.

Left at 7 in the morning. Arrived in Grasley at 9:30. Stayed to wait for the guide and camels behind us. Ate lunch. Got going at 1 o'clock. Arrived in Boyussa at 5:30. Impossible to cross the river. Camped with Monsieur Donald, his wife and 2 children.

Rain. Impossible to take off before 11 o'clock. The camels refused to be loaded. The stretcher left anyway and arrived in Voji in the rain at 2 o'clock. All evening and all night we waited for the camels which never came.

It rained for 16 hours straight and we had no provisions or tent. I passed the time beneath an Abyssinian skin.

Saturday the 11th.

On Saturday the 11th at 6 o'clock I sent 8 men to search for the camels and I stayed with the rest while waiting in Voji. The camels arrived at 4 in the afternoon and we ate after 30 hours of complete fasting, of which we were left without any shelter for 16 hours in the rain.

Sunday the 12th.

Left Voji at 6 o'clock. Passed through Cotto at 8:30. Stopped at the river in Dalahmaley, 10:40. Left again at 2 o'clock. Camped in Dalahmaley at 4:30... freezing. The camels didn't arrive until 6 in the evening.

Monday the 13th.

Left at 5:30. Arrived in Biokobobo at 9 o'clock. Camped.

Tuesday the 14th.

Left at 5:30. The carriers did a bad job. At 9:30, stopped in Arrowina. They tossed me to the ground when we got there. I imposed a 4-thaler fine: Mouned-Souyn, 1 thaler; Abdullahi, 1 thaler; Abdullah, 1 thaler; Bakir, 1 thaler. Left at 2 o'clock. Arrived in Samado at 5:30.

Wednesday the 15th.

Left at 6 o'clock. Arrived in Lasman at 10 o'clock. Got going again at 2:30. Arrived in Kombavoren at 6:30.

Thursday the 16th.

Left, 5:30. Passed Hensa. Stopped in Doudouhassa at 9 o'clock. Found $10^{1}/2$ daboulahs of coffee there for 1 rupee. Left, 2 o'clock. Dadap, 6:15. Found $5^{1}/2$ camels, 22 daboulahs of coffee and 11 skins: Adaouli.

Friday the 17th.

Left Dadap 9:30. Arrived in Warambot at 4:30.

Letter to Ras Mékonène, Governor of Harar[34]

Marseille, May 30, 1891.

Your Excellence,

How do you do? I wish you good health and complete prosperity. May God grant you all that you desire. May your existence flow peacefully.

I write to you from Marseille in France. I am in the hospital. Six days ago my leg was cut off. I am currently doing well and will be healed in about twenty days.

In a few months, I plan on returning to Harar to conduct trade as before, and I thought I would send my greetings to you.

Your devoted servant,

Rimbaud

from absinthe to abyssinia

END NOTES

1. "Zounds": This work, often attributed the title "Le Soleil était encore chaud" (the sun was still warm) as well as other titles (i.e., "Prologue," "Narration"), was written by Rimbaud when he was about ten years old. There is some debate as to Rimbaud's actual age at the time of this composition, but it is generally agreed that this piece was written between 1862 and 1865.

   Throughout this theme, written as a class assignment, Rimbaud plays with different forms of the word "saper-lipoppete," an exclamation with religious connotations. Whereas Oliver Bernard has translated this expression as "'sgibbet," "'steeth," "'sdeaths," and "'swounds," I picked the oath *Zounds* (an evolution of *God's wounds*), but chose not to play with its forms as much as Rimbaud did, the options being more limited in the English language.

   This piece is also interesting for its irony and serendipity: Rimbaud states that he finds languages like Latin useless, yet he goes on to win awards in Latin composition as well as study many different languages on his own. He also declares that he will be a rich man, an ambition he eventually aspires to, but runs into complications with in Abyssinia, where he pursues journalism.

2. "Dead Baby": This poem, commonly known as "L'Ange et l'enfant," was based on a poem by J. Reboul and composed in Latin by Rimbaud at the age of fourteen. Since it's not certain if Rimbaud ever titled the work himself, the title in this translation was attributed by the translator, as other translators have done in the past.

3. "Jesus of Nazareth": This Latin composition was also an

from absinthe to abyssinia

assignment for school. It was published in the *Bulletin de l'Académie de Douai*, as were many works written by Rimbaud during his time at the Collège de Charleville.

4. "Invocation to Venus": This poem was originally published in 1870, when Rimbaud was fifteen years old. This work, however, is a plagiarism of a Lucretius translation by Sully-Prudhomme, in which Rimbaud improved upon the language then passed the work off as his own.

5. "Three Kisses": This poem is the earliest known version of a poem later appearing under other titles (for example, "Première soirée" and "Comédie en trois baisers"), differing slightly in text each time it was published. This particular version was published in 1870.

6. "Scraps": All versions of "Bribes" (scraps) collected in the œuvres of Rimbaud seem to differ, either by the addition or the absence of a strophe or two. The reason for this has to do with all the editors who altered Rimbaud's poetry back in the nineteenth century, as well as some meddling by Paul Verlaine himself. Historically, different publications of Rimbaud's works have always contained minor deviations.

The dots (. . . . .), commonly found in works by Rimbaud, were installed by editors. They usually denote missing words.

7. The second "Scrap": Desdouets was the headmaster of the Collège de Charleville; Jean Baudry was a pseudonym for Rimbaud; and Jean Balouche was a pseudonym for his friend Ernest Delahaye. According to an ambiguous footnote in the translations of Oliver Bernard (which is almost

as ambiguous as the chamberpot), the belfry was ambiguous because "Rimbaud found a chamber-pot in it, which he hurled down on to the square" (See Rimbaud, Arthur. *Rimbaud: Collected Poems*. Trans. Oliver Bernard. New York: Penguin Books, 1986, p. 175, fn2).

8. The Universe: There used to be a bar/café in Charleville called L'Universe, where poets would read their work aloud.

9. "Reconstructed Scraps": These scraps were pieced together from torn poems by the Rimbaud scholar Alain Borer.

One interpretation of the "cloaky overcoats" who protect "a musky butt" is that Rimbaud is referring to bourgeois colleagues who defended his poetics in Paris.

Also, the following two lines ("as vulcanized leggings/ truss up a fat knee") could be considered prophetic in that Rimbaud died from a swollen knee — or rather, the complications of rheumatism which led to an amputation prompting his death.

The rest of this poem raises other questions, particularly on the use of some of the more heavy-handed multi-syllabic words that are not considered consistent with Rimbaud's poetic vocabulary at the time. One possibility is that this poem was derived from an experimental collaboration (such as the post-Dada writing game *le cadavre exquis*), which wasn't an uncommon practice among the emerging pre-Surrealists of the era.

10. *Damninetics*: *Album zutique*, or *Album dit <<zutique>>*, was a collaboration by the members of a club of lewd poets who drank absinthe and smoked hashish in the dark recesses of underground Paris where they made fun of each others'

poetry. This club included Rimbaud, Verlaine, François Coppée and more.

As is the case with "Scraps," there are discrepancies between the various existing texts of this work, some containing strophes and lines that other editions left out, and all editions differing in the order of arrangement.

The myth about *Album zutique* is that there had been a mysterious third manuscript of Rimbaud's that had gone unaccounted for well into the twentieth century. This manuscript was discovered during World War II and ended up in the hands of Marc Barbezat, the publisher of L'Arbalète, a small press on the outskirts of Lyon. Along with James Joyce's *Ulysses*, which Sylvia Beach was publishing up in Paris, and other works of art considered threatening to the Third Reich, the Nazis demanded *Album zutique*. Barbezat, however, was also the publisher of the legendary poet-thief Jean Genet, who went to Lyon and stole the original manuscript, then sold it to some shifty dealer on the Seine. The type had been set though, and the work was printed and distributed secretly.

"Zutique," an adjective derived from the exclamation "Zut!", basically means *Goddammit!* Thus, the title *Daminetics*, a parody of a parody, was arrived at by the translator.

11. "Young Glutton": The "baguette" being prepared by Verlaine is also slang for *cock*.

12. "Parody of Louis-Xavier de Ricard": Rimbaud is mocking Louis-Xavier de Ricard's *La Revue du progrès moral* and its religious ideals.

According to Claude Jeancolas, the image of Humanity

putting shoes on the personification of Progress alludes to an erotic analogy of unbridled homosexuality (See Jeancolas, Claude. *Le Dictionnaire Rimbaud*. Paris: Éditions Balland, 1991, p. 72).

13. "Fête Galante": Rimbaud is playing with the word "lapin" (rabbit), which refers to a person of passion and virility and is also a play on "la pine" (slang for *penis*). "Lapin" can also mean *an old war hero, a casanova,* or *nymphomaniac.*

    Scapin was an Italian stage-clown. Colombina, the daughter of Harlequin and Cassandra, was also a character from the Italian comedies.

    The overcoat (or raincoat), as in English, is slang for *condom.*

    "Tapin," vernacular for *slut,* is also a verb for *hide.*

    This poem can therefore be interpreted in many ways.

14. "Coppée Copy": The capitalized noun "Filet" (translated here as "Channel") has been baffling translators of Rimbaud for over half a century. On one hand it refers to the phallic tubeway, but on the other hand it can be combined with "d'eau" (which follows it in the poem), thus forming an idiom for *stream of water.*

15. "State of Siege?": Rimbaud's use of the word "omnibus" (a fancy multi-tiered carriage) in this poem includes the secondary meaning of a *fat whore* (see Jeancolas, pp. 199–200).

16. "Old Guard": This term refers to the old soldiers of Napoleon's Empire who were supposedly reincarnated in the Paris Commune which began on March 18, 1871, when Napoleon III was freed from captivity. Two days before that, Empress Eugénie gave birth to his son.

17. "Potty Poetry": Rimbaud is playing with the word "siege," which translates as "seat" and includes the context of *toilet, throne*, and *seat of power*. "Siege" also refers to a *military siege*, or *coup*, especially in the first line.

   Henri Kinck was a six-year-old boy, massacred along with seven other family members by Troppmann in 1869.

   Henry V reigned for one day in 1830 and Napoleon III seized the power of the presidency in 1851 through a coup d'état, but fell from power in 1870.

18. "Wastelands of Love": These poems were written in 1871. There is some confusion about the order of the last two sections, which have been published (as well as translated) in differing orders. According to the Rimbaud editor Suzanne Bernard (See Rimbaud, Arthur. *Œuvres de Rimbaud*. Paris: Éditions Garnier Frères, 1960, p. 188, fn8), all versions of this poem preceding 1957 were published with the piece beginning "Cette fois c'est la Femme..." following the preface. Why sections got switched around is open to speculation. This translation, however, chooses to go with the pre-1957 order, because it's logical for the narrator's disillusionment to begin with a girl in the country then move on to Woman in the City.

19. "Rough Drafts": "Ébauches" (also known as "Evangelical Prose," and usually referred to individually as "À Samarie," "En Galilée," and "Bethsaïda, la piscine") has a long history of misinterpretation. First off, Rimbaud editors once believed that "Bethsaïda" was the lost prelude to *Une Saison en enfer*, because it was found scrawled on the back of a manuscript. This idea was later refuted as the argument arose that if

Rimbaud wanted "Ébauches" to be a prelude to *Saison*, then he would have had the book published with these poems as the prelude, since he printed it at his own expense anyway.

Also, many typographical errors have resulted from Rimbaud's often indecipherable handwriting. The most famous of these errors occurred with the word "Beth-Saïda," which was believed to be "Cette saison" for decades.

Whereas "Bethsaïda, la piscine" was first published in *La Revue blanche* in 1897, "À Samarie" and "En Galilée" remained missing until 1948 when they were both published by Mercure de France.

These poems, all based on the life of Jesus according to "The Book of John," were abandoned by Rimbaud and never revised to a level of craftmanship consistent with his other works of poetry.

20. "Sketches of *Season in Hell*": These rough outlines for *Une Saison en enfer* were discovered one piece at a time (first in 1897, then in 1914, and then in 1948), but do not comprise the entire collection of "Brouillons" (or sketches), of which a few sections were left out of these translations.

These works were written at the same time as "Rough Drafts." In both "Rough Drafts" and "Sketches" there are missing words and incomplete, incoherent sentences with many mistranscriptions. Hence, translating these pieces involved some reconstruction through extrapolation while referring to words that were once crossed out according to the notes in the Pléiade edition of the œuvres.

Like quite a few other pieces by Rimbaud, the "Sketches" also contain instances that could be considered prophetic in that they foreshadow the geographical and emotional destinations Rimbaud is heading for (i.e., "Let's go! The desert, the burden, the violence, misfortune, the anger and ennui").

21. "Vi(o)lations": These sonnets, known as "Les Stupra," were written in collaboration with Verlaine. The Latin "stupra" is plural for *stuprum,* which means an obscene and/or illegitimate copulation. Past translators have called these poems "Defilements" and "Scatological Poems." These translations, however, employ the neologism "Vi(o)lations" because it joins the context of *vile* with the context of *rape.*

Since the third "Vi(o)lation" is commonly referred to as "The Asshole Sonnet" in English, the other stupra were attributed titles by the translator according to their subject matter.

In "The Cock Sonnet," Kleber refers to a celebrated French general whose well-endowed effigy was prominently displayed on the facade of the Louvre.

22. "Dream": This poem, included in a personal correspondence of 1875, is the last known poem Rimbaud ever wrote. François-Joseph Lefebvre (1755–1820) was a Marshal of France and Keller was François Kellermann, who lived during the same time and held the same title.

In French, the word "génie" can mean *genie* as well as *genius.* No doubt, Rimbaud meant to allude to both of these possibilities as well as his own concept of the word, which he illustrates in the last poem of *Illuminations.*

23. "Fragment from a Letter to Verlaine": This partial letter is one of twelve letters sometimes referred to as "Lettres martyriques." The other letters are supposedly lost.

24. Statements to the Police: Whereas other legal testimonies of Rimbaud and Verlaine have been translated into English regarding the incident in Brussels when Verlaine shot Rimbaud, these statements have never been seen in English prior to these translations. Verlaine's statement was included here to show both sides of the story.

25. "Letter to the American Consul": This letter, originally written in English, remains unedited. It should also be mentioned that Rimbaud's math was a little off: he was not 5-foot-6, he was 5-foot-11. Also, Rimbaud was never in the 47th Regiment, but his father was.

26. It is rumored that Rimbaud was the first European to explore the Abyssinian region, but this is false. Sir Richard Francis Burton visited Harar in 1855, followed by two Italians and then a Greek named Sotiro. The latter collected most of the information Rimbaud used in this commercial and geographical report written for Alfred Bardey, Rimbaud's employer at the time.

The purpose of the report was to evaluate the possibilities for setting up trading posts in the Ogaden, but Rimbaud was also aware of the possibility of obtaining funds for further exploration from the Sociéte de Géographie, which published this piece in their proceedings. Rimbaud is often criticized by his biographers for not following up on requests later made by the Society, which could have led to further opportunities for publication and exploration. Squabbles over money disillusioned Rimbaud and he never responded to their letters.

The "Report on the Ogaden," aside from its wealth of information on the territory, is interesting for the changes it shows in the post-Paris Rimbaud. As he strove to disassociate himself from the "decadent poets" of France by focusing on subjects he considered to be more scientific, his style became more serious, flat, and even purposefully sloppy at times — but still, not without a sense for assonance, alliteration and other techniques practiced in his poetry.

27. "To the *Bosphore Égyptien*": This work is the longest known work written by Rimbaud after leaving Europe. Rimbaud wrote it for an Egyptian newspaper when he visited Cairo in 1887. It is somewhat similar to the Ogaden report, containing information on the political and economic climate of Abyssinia and other African regions. King Ménélik is mentioned quite frequently, along with his Dedjatch (military leader) Mékonène.

As a side note, it is unlikely that Rimbaud really carved his name on the pyramid wall in the Valley of the Sphinxes when he visited Egypt, as legend has it. Rimbaud was not a vandal and has never been known for leaving such insignias anywhere, especially after he left Europe. In Abyssinia, it was Rimbaud's desire to remain inconspicuous rather than call attention to himself; he took measures to conceal his past from his associates and resisted all appeals by the Paris literati calling him back to France. Besides, these inscriptions were "discovered" by the famous myth-maker Jean Cocteau in 1949, just a few years after he petitioned the President of France to free Jean Genet from a life sentence in prison on the grounds that "He is Rimbaud," and succeeded in the effort.

28. "Letter to Vice Consul Gaspary": Rimbaud was business partners with Monsieur Labatut who died while traveling in Africa. This letter addresses the debts and the problems with paying their balance that the tragedy caused. It's a

bumbling, ridiculous comedy of desperate creditors and money-moochers in primitive Africa.

The Azzaze he keeps referring to is a native official in charge of servants and domestic affairs, who oversees business deals and local judicial matters.

29. Letters to Ilg: Alfred Ilg was a Swiss official in the employment of King Ménélik, in charge of managing transactions with the Europeans for the royal Abyssinian court. Rimbaud wrote prolifically to Ilg, perhaps more than to anybody else in the 1880s. At first these letters were amusing and slightly ribald, as they were clearly meant to entertain the reader in order to gain his favor. In the end, however, they show Rimbaud's irritation and impatience in his business dealings with the King.

30. Letters to Ugo Ferrandi: Ferrandi was an Italian explorer who traveled with Rimbaud. Many of these letters do not appear in the œuvres because, like other letters included in this collection, they were discovered after the œuvres were compiled. No doubt, there are more letters still out there waiting to be found, released to the public or sold to collectors.

31. "Letter to King Ménélik": When doing business with the King, Rimbaud almost always went through Ilg. In this case, though, Rimbaud's needs were not being met, so he decided to go over Ilg's head by entrusting Ilg with a letter for Ménélik. Not surprisingly, the letter was never delivered.

32. "Letter to Armand Savouré": Savouré was a colleague of Rimbaud, also trading in Africa. He responded to this tirade

(which is thought to be written in April 1890) by dismissing Rimbaud's reaction as a typical exaggeration, explaining that the reason for the poor quality of his coffee had to do with pressure from bandits — a subject Rimbaud was personally familiar with.

33. "Notes of the Damned": Whereas Rimbaud never titled this work, the translator did, deriving the title from Alain Borer who referred to this piece as Rimbaud's "carnet de damné," a phrase taken from the last line of the first section of *Season in Hell*. It's a record of his journey on a stretcher across the desert, en route to the coast.

The pain in Rimbaud's leg can almost be felt in the sparsity of words in this piece, clearly written for purposes other than pleasure. It is constructed through partial sentences and phrases awkwardly mixing past and present tenses together — a characteristic this translation opted to improve upon for the sake of consistency and easier reading.

It is believed that the "chx" used in the entry on the 16th refers to camels. Still, the number $5^1/2$ is an unlikely number, so could perhaps refer to something else. Some scholars believe that Rimbaud was either greatly distracted by his pain at this point, or was entering a state of delirium.

34. "Letter to Ras Mékonène": Rimbaud wrote this letter from his death-bed, no doubt in a great deal of pain, to assure his position in Abyssinia upon his return.

But Rimbaud did not return. He died November 10, 1891, after dictating his last letter, a mysterious list of elephant tusks followed by a delusionary business letter requesting passage to Suez from a mysterious place called Aphinar.

Sources

"Prologue": *Œuvres Rimbaud*. Ed. Suzanne Bernard. Paris: Garnier Frères, 1960, pp. 5–7.

"Invocation à Vénus": *Vers de collège*. Ed. Jules Mouquet. Paris: Mercure de France, 1932, p. 68.

"L'Ange et l'enfant": *Ibid.*, pp. 32–37.

"Jésus à Nazareth": *Ibid.*, pp. 56–61.

"Trois baisers": *Œuvres-vie*. Ed. Alain Borer. Paris: Arléa, 1991, pp. 100–101.

"Bribes": *Œuvres complètes*. Eds. Rolland de Renéville and Jules Mouquet. Paris: Éditions Gallimard, 1951, pp. 106–108.

"Iranian caravan": *Œuvres complètes*. Ed. Antoine Adam. Paris: Éditions Gallimard, 1972, pp. 222–223.

"Bouts-rimés reconstitués, par Alain Borer": *Œuvres-vie*, pp. 857–858.

"Jeune goinfre": *Œuvres complètes*, 1972, p. 210.

"Cocher ivre": *Ibid.*, pp. 211–212.

"Les Lèvres closes vu à Rome": *Ibid.*, p. 208.

"L'Angelot maudit": *Ibid.*, p. 213.

"Lys": *Ibid.*, p. 208.

"L'Humanité": *Ibid.*, p. 210.

"Fête galante": *Ibid.*, p. 209.

"Les Remembrances du vieillard idiot": *Ibid.*, pp. 215–217.

"Les Soirs d'été...": *Ibid.*, p. 214.

"État de siège": *Ibid.*, p. 212.

"Hypotyposes saturniennes, ex Belmontet": *Ibid.*, p. 215.

"Vieux de la vieille": *Ibid.*, p. 212.

"Vers pour les lieux": *Ibid.*, p. 219.

"Le Bateau ivre": *Poésies.* Ed. H. de Bouillane de Lacoste. Paris: Mercure de France, 1947, pp. 175–179.

"Les Déserts de l'amour": *Œuvres de Arthur Rimbaud.* Ed. Patern Berrichon. Paris: Mercure de France, 1934, pp. 101–107.

"Ébauches I & II": *Œuvres de Arthur Rimbaud.* Paris: Mercure de France, 1952, pp. 203–204.

"Ébauche III": *Œuvres de Arthur Rimbaud,* 1934, pp. 251–253.

"Brouillons d'*Une Saison en enfer*": *Œuvres complètes,* 1972, pp. 165–167.

Une Saison en enfer: Montreal: Les Éditions Variétés, 1946, pp. 9–17.

"Les Stupra": *Œuvres complètes,* 1951, pp. 109–110.

"Bottom": *Œuvres de Arthur Rimbaud,* 1952, p. 261.

"Rêve": *Œuvres complètes,* 1972, p. 299.

Part II

Letter, April 1872: *Œuvre-vie*, p. 283.

"Déclaration de Rimbaud au commissaire de police": *Arthur Rimbaud: Œuvres complètes, correspondance*. Ed. Louis Forestier. Paris: Robert Laffont, 1992, p. 383.

"Déclaration de Verlaine au commissaire de police": *Ibid.*, p. 384.

"Rimbaud au Consul des États-Unis d'Amérique à Brême": *Œuvres complètes*, 1972, pp. 302–303.

"Rapport sur l'Ogadine": *Arthur Rimbaud: "Je suis ici dans les Gallas."* Ed. Alain Jouffroy. Monaco: Éditions du Rocher, 1991, pp. 51–58.

Letter, December 21, 1883: *Œuvres complètes: Correspondance*. Lausanne, Switzerland: Henri Kaeser, 1943, p. 176.

"Rimbaud au Directeur du <<Bosphore égyptien>>": *Œuvres complètes*, 1972, pp. 430–440.

Letter, November 9, 1887: *Œuvres complètes*, 1972, pp. 461–466.

Letter, February 1, 1888: *Correspondance: 1888–1891*. Ed. Jean Voellmy. Paris: Éditions Gallimard, 1965, pp. 52–57.

Letter, March 29, 1888: *Ibid.*, pp. 62–64.

Letter, April 2, 1888: *Commentaires, transcriptions et chemine-*

ments des manuscrits. Ed. Claude Jeancolas. Paris: Les Éditions Textuel, 1997, p. 456.

Letter, April 4, 1888: *Ibid.,* p. 457.

Letter, April 10, 1888: *Ibid.*

Letter, April 12, 1888: *Correspondance: 1888–1891,* pp. 64–65.

Letter, April 30, 1889: *Commentaires, transcriptions et cheminements des manuscrits,* p. 463.

Letter, September 7, 1889: *Correspondance: 1888–1891,* pp. 105–114.

Letter, September 18, 1889: *Ibid.,* pp. 121–122.

Letters, October 7 & 9, 1889: *Ibid.,* pp. 123–129.

Letter, December 11, 1889: *Ibid.,* pp. 144–145.

Letter, January 3, 1890: *Commentaires, transcriptions et cheminements des manuscrits,* pp. 501–502.

Letter, April 7, 1890: *Correspondance: 1888–1891,* pp. 167–168.

Letter, April 1890: *Œuvres complètes,* 1972, pp. 626–627.

Letter, September 20, 1890: *Correspondance: 1888–1891,* pp. 189–193.

Letter, November 20, 1890: *Ibid.,* pp. 199–201.

"Itinéraire de Harar à Warambot": *Œuvres complètes,* 1972, pp. 659–661.

Letter, May 30, 1891: *Œuvres complètes,* 1972, p. 668.

MARK SPITZER has degrees in creative writing from the University of Minnesota, the University of Colorado, and Louisiana State University. He is the translator of *The Collected Poems of Georges Bataille* (Dufour Editions, 1998), and co-translator of *The Church*, by Louis-Ferdinand Céline (Green Integer, 2002). He has also translated Jean Genet, Blaise Cendrars, and other works by Céline and Bataille. His novels include *Bottom Feeder* (Creative Arts, 1999) and *Chum* (Zoland Books, 2001). He currently lives in Baton Rouge, where he is Assistant Editor of *Exquisite Corpse* (www.corpse.org).